Contents

£3·95

Studying

© 1988 Ruth Sherry

First published in Great Britain 1988

British Library Cataloguing in Publication Data

Sherry, Ruth
    Studying women's writing : an introduction.
    1. Western literatures. Women writers —
    Critical studies
    I. Title
    809'.89287

    ISBN 0–7131–6566–9

Typeset in 10/11pt Cheltenham Book Compugraphic
by Colset Private Ltd, Singapore
Printed and bound in Great Britain
for Edward Arnold, the educational academic and medical
publishing division of Hodder and Stoughton Limited,
41 Bedford Square, London WC1B 3DQ by Richard Clay plc,
Bungay, Suffolk

26. 1. 89

1 What is Women's Writing?

Is there such a thing as women's literature?

Often the first question that is asked, if one talks about studying women's literature, is, 'Why *women's* literature? Isn't all literature fundamentally the same?'

There is no absolute answer to a question like this. Certainly there are many literary texts which a reader could look at without being able to tell whether they were written by a woman or a man. In all cultures that we know of, however, the lives and experiences of men and women are different in many ways. It would be surprising if such differences were not reflected in some degree in what men write and what women write.

We are not usually made uncomfortable by the idea that it is useful, for purposes of studying, to divide literature into categories which emphasize one significant aspect of the texts we are considering. We may find it helpful to read sixteenth-century works separately from nineteenth-century works, to consider poetry separately from fiction, to look at Irish or Canadian literature separately from literature written by British authors. Especially in recent years, many people have felt that it is similarly useful to look at works written by women separately from works written by men. Some approaches which have traditionally been used in studying all literature may really not be very relevant to works written by women.

If we consider, for example, a novel by Jane Austen in the light of the fact that the author was a woman, we are not prohibited from also, at another time, thinking of it as an English (not American) novel, or as an early nineteenth-century (not mid eighteenth-century) work.

In the past, works which focus on women were often thought of as aimed mainly at women readers, while works which focus on men were considered to be aimed at a 'general' audience, suitable for reading and study by both men and women. It has not usually been considered particularly significant that a major novel like Herman Melville's *Moby Dick* (1851) has no women characters. Some subjects (waging war, life at sea, struggles for political power) seem to exclude or minimize women characters because for the most part women have not, historically, been central or public participants in these activities. Thus Joseph Conrad's *The Secret Sharer* (1910) or Stephen Crane's *The Red Badge of Courage* (1895) are not regarded as unusual or narrow in their focus even though their characters are drawn from only one-half of the human race, yet Clare Boothe's Broadway comedy, *The Women* (1936), was thought remarkable in its time because all the characters were women. Yet it should not be surprising that literature written by women focuses on women characters, on women's lives and experiences.

The judgement that works about men are 'general' while works about women are 'narrow' or 'specialized' tells us something about the way in which our culture has evaluated the relative importance of the experience of men and the experience of women. As this evaluation changes, we notice that women writers frequently have given us a more detailed depiction of women's lives, ideas, emotions and preoccupations, than men have. Perhaps, in works by women, there are relatively few male characters, or they occupy a less central place than the women characters do.

Of course, relatively few writers confine themselves entirely to writing about the experiences of one sex only, and men have often written about women, just as most women writers include both sexes in their fiction and drama. Shakespeare's plays, for example, have an overwhelming predominance of male characters, but in many of them the few women who appear are of central importance. In England especially, a number of male novelists, including Samuel Richardson, Daniel Defoe and George Meredith, have written major novels in which the central character is a woman; this phenomenon is especially common in the eighteenth and nineteenth centuries. In this period, a great many English novels had plots which involved an attractive and marriageable young woman and her adventures (or misadventures) on the way to the altar. However, in these works written by men, the women characters are almost always seen primarily in relation to men, and they are usually of interest largely in terms of their romantic and sexual relationships.

Women writers likewise often treat problems of love, sexuality and marriage, but women writers frequently include other aspects of women's lives as well. Perhaps there are relatively few male characters, or they occupy a less central place in the work than the women characters do. In Charlotte Brontë's *Jane Eyre* (1847), for example, we are given detailed treatments of Jane's relationships with two men, Mr Rochester and St John Rivers. Although both of these are certainly central to the novel, Charlotte Brontë also gives detailed accounts of Jane's relationships with a number of female characters: Mrs Reed, Eliza and Georgianna, Helen Burns, Miss Temple, Mrs Fairfax, Diana and Mary Rivers. Considerable attention is given to Jane's reading, to her education and her interest in art, and there is some account of her activities as a teacher.

Virginia Woolf's novel *Mrs Dalloway* (1925) presents a day in the life of a middle-aged married woman who is a political hostess giving an evening party. Close attention is given to Mrs Dalloway's responsibilities and plans as a hostess – buying flowers, arranging for food and drink, conferring with servants, planning her own clothing, bringing her guests together during the party. Many of her activities may at first glance seem insignificant, but here and elsewhere (in *To the Lighthouse* (1927) for example) Woolf underlines the ways in which apparently trivial tasks performed by a woman make it possible for other characters to lead fulfilling lives in comfortable circumstances. The political decision-making process, ostensibly a male activity, is shown as depending partly upon well-run parties like that given by Mrs Dalloway and her rival, Lady Bruton.

In addition Woolf presents Mrs Dalloway's own emotional life and memories, as well as those of other characters. Although Mrs Dalloway is white-haired and has a heart condition, she is still the object of romantic attention from, among others, her husband and her former suitor, Peter Walsh. She still responds strongly to memories of certain crucial encounters. Here Woolf helps to dismantle the stereotype that women are romantically and emotionally interesting only when they are young and mainly when they are unmarried.

Mrs Dalloway is notable partly because of its use of imagery, often drawn from everyday life, to present the characters' mental processes. At one point, Mrs Dalloway is shown mending a dress – threading a needle, using a thimble, gathering material. In the context this activity represents the general idea of restoring and maintaining order, but the use of such images, drawn from a woman's actual everyday activities, probably would not occur to a man writing.

Tillie Olsen's *Yonnondio: From the Thirties* (1974) treats a working-class American family and focuses particularly on the difficulties for women of trying to cope with poverty, bad housing and illness. The novel shows the energy, stamina and determination required for a woman to keep a minimal basic family life going against virtually impossible odds. Typically, the demands on such a woman's attention are myriad and unrelenting, and even when she is ill a mother feels constant responsibility for all the small but essential elements of everyday life.

One passage shows Anna juggling and balancing such responsibilities. In the middle of a heat wave she must cope with several children, including one baby who is sick, at the same time as cooking peaches for preserving because only at this time are they plentiful and cheap.

The last batch of jelly is on the stove. Between stirring and skimming, and changing the wet packs on Ben, Anna peels and cuts the canning peaches – two more lugs to go. If only all will sleep awhile. She begins to sing softly – *I saw a ship a-sailing, a-sailing on the sea* – it clears her head. The drone of fruit flies and Ben's rusty breathing are very loud in the unmoving heavy air. Bess begins to fuss again. *There, there, Bessie, there, there,* stopping to sponge down the oozing sores on the tiny body. *There.* Skim, stir; sprinkle Bess; pit, peel and cut; sponge; skim, stir. Any second the jelly will be right and must not wait. Shall she wake up Jimmie and ask him to blow a feather to keep Bess quiet? No, he'll wake up cranky, he's just a baby hisself, let him sleep. Skim, stir; sprinkle; change the wet packs on Ben; pit, peel and cut; sponge. This time it does not soothe – Bess stiffens her body, flails her fists, begins to scream in misery. Just then the jelly begins to boil. There is nothing for it but to take Bess up, jounce her on a hip *(there, there)* and with her one free hand frantically skim and ladle. *There,*

there. The batch is poured and capped and sealed, all one-handed, jiggling-hipped. There, there, it is done.[1]

Olsen shows Anna's thoughts and activities as being virtually a miracle of organization and, not least, physical skill and co-ordination. Women readers will certainly recognize the situation of trying to cope with something boiling in a pot while balancing a baby on the hip. It is not, perhaps, strictly impossible that a man could have written such a passage, but surely it is far more likely to have come from a woman.

Literature, and the arts in general, can be thought of as having many different functions, but one thing which most readers look for in literature, at least some of the time, is some reflection of their own experiences. Most of us, automatically and almost unthinkingly, check what we observe, feel and experience against the observations of others, and we need to know that our experiences and perceptions are at least to some degree shared or understood by others. If we find that our experiences and perceptions are shared by other people, we say that these are 'authenticated'. While there are many ways in which we can find this authentication, reading works of literature is one of them. Similarly, if we feel that the experiences and perceptions reflected in a literary work are ones which we can recognize, or at least understand and accept as human, we are likely to say that the work is 'authentic'.

To say that we often look to literature to authenticate our experience is not necessarily the same thing as saying that literature should preferably be about experiences which are typical, or very widely shared. In fact, experiences or responses which are *not* commonplace are often the impetus for literary writing; perhaps a few readers will recognize these while others will have their understanding of human possibility and variety enlarged. However, there are some groups of people who are in particular need of having their experiences shared with others. These include the many groups in society whose lives have been largely ignored by the general public culture, which includes the popular press, television and film as well as drama and other literature. Such groups include racial, ethnic and religious minorities, handicapped people and the elderly. Social psychologists refer to such groups as having their experience 'marginalized' – that is, it is not seen as central, fundamental, typical or normal for the society in which they live. Being regarded as marginal is a source of psychological stress, often leading to a feeling of power-lessness and lack of a secure sense of identity.

Women are not numerically a minority in our society – usually something slightly over 50 per cent of the population is female, in Western societies – but in many respects women's lives, experiences and values have been treated as marginal and men's experiences have been assumed to be normative. In addition, there has been a general tendency to assume that 'important' activities are those which occur in the public sphere, while private life and feelings are less important, of concern only to the individuals involved. Literature about public events has thus often been thought to be somehow more serious, more weighty, than that about private life. This assumption can easily lead to the result that literature by and about women is undervalued or dismissed. As Virginia Woolf observed in *A Room of One's Own* (1929), a common judge-ment was 'This is an important book . . . because it deals with war. This is an insignificant book because it deals with the feel-ings of women in a drawing room.'[2]

Such evaluations are now increasingly questioned and rejected. The experience of women – of more than half of the population – is surely as important as that of men. A dis-tinction between 'public' and 'private' activity is artificial. Per-haps it is mostly men who decide to declare wars and who fight in them, but women lose homes and families in wars and may very well be killed themselves.

For women, reading literary works in which their own experiences are reflected can be an important authentication of that experience, and of their own identity and values. For men, reading literary works by women can often provide insights, perhaps sometimes surprising ones, about those with whom they share the planet and, probably, their daily lives.

Women writing about women

We have already noted that women are particularly well placed to write about the daily lives and activities of women, and may give more attention to women characters than male writers do. And, as we have seen in *Jane Eyre*, women writers are often especially interested in relationships between women. Certainly not all treatments of such female relation-ships are positive – Jane Eyre is badly treated by her aunt and her cousins Eliza and Georgianna – but frequently works by women unobtrusively record how important women are in each others' lives. We know, for example, that Jane Austen had a very close relationship with her sister Cassandra. In *Pride and Prejudice* (1813), Jane and Elizabeth similarly provide companionship and support for each other in a family other-wise made up of rather unsatisfactory individuals, and they are much helped by the affection of their Aunt Gardiner.

Charlotte Brontë does not give any of the main female char-acters in her novels a sister, yet surely the shared intellectual and artistic life of the three Brontë sisters provided her with an awareness of how central such female relationships could be – and, conversely, how desolate life might be without them. The 'happy ending' of *Jane Eyre* does not consist only in Jane's reunion with Mr Rochester; it also includes her regaining a family which includes two young women who are Jane's moral and intellectual equals.

More recent women writers are often explicit in showing that friendships between women can be characterized by openness, trust, intellectual stimulation and long-term stability which women frequently find difficult to achieve in relation-ships with men. Doris Lessing's *The Golden Notebook* (1962) gives great attention to the relationships of the protagonist, Anna, with her various lovers, yet it is her friendship with Molly which provides a frame for the novel and, for Anna, something akin to the permanence which is, at best, found in family life.

More openness in recent years has also encouraged the pub-lication of a number of novels and poems based on a lesbian outlook, and has also directed attention to lesbian elements in the work of long-established writers such as Virginia Woolf and Willa Cather. For lesbian writers such as the poet Adrienne Rich, relationships between women are, naturally, not merely important, but crucial.

We are well aware that there is a considerable literature by men about sons and fathers (Ivan Turgenev's *Fathers and Sons* is merely the most obvious example), and almost equally extensive literature about sons and mothers (D. H. Lawrence's *Sons and Lovers* coming most readily to mind). Themes, such as that of the Oedipus complex, with which we are very familiar, are often thought of as 'universal', although in fact they apply only to the experience of sons. That daughters' relationships with their parents are equally central is of course obvious when one thinks about it for a moment, and several recent writers have pointed to the fact that a significant literature on this subject must be created by women themselves. To some extent it already exists, Elizabeth Gaskell's *Wives and Daughters* (1866) providing a case in point. Some of the most famous literary treatments of this theme are negative, as in Sylvia Plath's representation of her father as an oppressor in her poem 'Daddy', and of her mother as ambitious and insensitive in her novel *The Bell Jar* (1963).

The black American writer Alice Walker, in her essay 'In Search of Our Mothers' Gardens' (1974), conversely celebrates what she has gained from her mother: a model of energy, nurturing and creative activity. Creative expression in the conventional artistic modes was not available to Walker's mother, but her aesthetic sense was expressed in the garden she cultivated, and Walker sees this example as part of her mother's legacy to her.

As we have already seen, all-male communities, including the military, ships at sea, boys' schools and men's colleges have provided extensive material for literature from as far back as we know – the time of Homer. Women's communities, such as those found in schools, colleges, convents and hospitals provide similar material. Many of the most widely-read works of this kind are detective stories (a genre to which women have made a notable and widely-recognized contribution), such as Dorothy L. Sayers's *Gaudy Night* (1935), Josephine Tey's *Miss Pym Disposes* (1946), and P. D. James's *Shroud for a Nightingale* (1971). Extensive treatments can be found in other kinds of fiction as well, such as Antonia White's semi-autobiographical novel about her school days, *Frost in May* (1935) and Julia O'Faolain's historical novel, *Women in the Wall* (1975), set in a convent in sixth-century Gaul.

Stories treating this material often have a double thrust. Within the community itself, women (abbesses, teachers, matrons) can provide authority figures and serve as models for girls or younger women. In all-female institutions, women fulfil a variety of functions and are allowed to develop skills and talents usually reserved for men in the larger world. At the same time, most of these women's institutions are shown in fiction as ultimately existing at the mercy of a male-dominated world, with figures such as policemen, clergymen, doctors and university officials free to intervene and assert a greater authority, especially in times of crisis.

In *Frost in May*, for example, girls are not educated primarily for intellectual achievement or financial independence. Rather, the aristocratic pupils are trained to be suitable wives for powerful men. Ironically, their teachers are nuns dedicated to poverty and chastity, but for all these girls and women, conformity and obedience are seen as the primary virtues. In *Women in the Wall*, the convent is rather seen as a woman's only retreat from a world of political power struggles, wars, bloodshed and sexual violence, but these forces can at any time invade the relative peace and seclusion of the convent world and bring disaster to the carefully created order within.

Of course women are also uniquely placed to write about their own sexuality. While an occasional writer in earlier centuries, such as the seventeenth-century poet and dramatist Aphra Behn, wrote fairly directly about women's sexual desires, for the most part this topic has been regarded as taboo for women writing in English until very recent times. Women like George Eliot (Mary Ann Evans), Emily Brontë and Emily Dickinson certainly wrote about passion, but its physical component was either left unstated or treated indirectly. Although earlier centuries had a rather more open attitude, the topic was also generally taboo for men writing for a mixed audience in the nineteenth century. Early in the twentieth century, however, men such as James Joyce and D. H. Lawrence produced highly-acclaimed works of considerable sexual frankness, yet serious women writers still generally felt obliged to avoid describing this aspect of life.

One result of this situation is that, until fairly recently, the best-known literary accounts of women's sexual experiences have come from men, whether in semi-pornographic works such as John Cleland's *Fanny Hill* (1748–9) or more solemn ones like D. H. Lawrence's *Lady Chatterley's Lover* (1928). Women writers and critics now feel free to say openly that these depictions by male writers often seem false or unconvincing to women. One of the first and most influential works in the current phase of feminist criticism, Kate Millett's *Sexual Politics* (1970), attacks literary representations of women's sexuality by several well-known male writers, some of whom were partly influenced by the theories of psychoanalysts, especially Sigmund Freud, whose theories of sexuality were essentially based on male, rather than female, responses. At worst, women may have questioned or rejected their own genuine sexual responses because these did not seem to be authenticated by the psychoanalytic explanations and literary representations given by men, and no corrective accounts authored by women were generally available. At the same time, men may have been seriously misled about what to expect from women.

Now, however, a considerable number of serious women writers have produced explicit depictions of sexual activity from a woman's point of view. Some of these have, at least initially, seemed shocking. One study found that male readers of Mary McCarthy's novel *The Group* (1963) tended to feel that the description given of sexual intercourse was 'sardonic and mocking', while women readers felt that it was merely realistic.[3] Much of Doris Lessing's *The Golden Notebook* is devoted to an explicit discussion of female sexual response and how it differs from what men expect or want (although many women readers in fact disagree with Lessing's own evaluations). In Alice Walker's *The Color Purple* (1982), one woman teaches another to observe and enjoy her own physical reactions. The New Zealand poet Fleur Adcock sardonically recommends the pleasures of masturbation in her poem 'Against Coupling' (1971).

There will probably always be some people who reject explicit representations of sexuality in any art form, and of course such material is so highly charged emotionally that it is not surprising that it seems threatening or dangerous to some. The erotic nevertheless forms a recurring and permanent part of the world's artistic legacy, and certainly if it is legitimate for men to represent sexual experience, it is equally legitimate for women to do so.

What else do women write about?

It is of course not the case that women write only about matters specific to themselves, or about private, rather than public, matters. Nor do women necessarily write, for example, novels in which the central characters are women. It is impossible to generalize adequately about the vast variety of work written by women, but it is nevertheless appropriate to ask whether we can identify any particular subjects or literary types to which significant numbers of women writers seem drawn.

It has long been noticed that there are certain areas of public concern in which women have been particularly likely to engage themselves. Among these are questions affecting children, such as education and infant health. Others are those which we might label as being matters of public morality, or those involving a social conscience, such as peace, human rights, nuclear disarmament and the abolition of slavery.

In Britain, many of the major social problems of the nineteenth century were caused by the interrelated processes of industrialization, migration and urbanization which led to the creation of an urban working class. A number of major writers treated these subjects more or less extensively in their work, including for example Charles Dickens in his novel *Hard Times* (1854), but in fact the first writers of fiction to take up this material were middle-class women. Among these were minor figures and several whose main energy was concentrated in other fields, such as Hannah More and Harriet Martineau.

The most famous of the women treating this material was unquestionably Elizabeth Gaskell, whose novels *Mary Barton* (1848) and *North and South* (1855) reflect the author's own middle-class standing but also insist upon the necessity for the middle classes to understand the lives and problems of the working classes. Gaskell's novels sometimes present working-class characters as morally superior to those of higher social standing, an idea Dickens picked up and used in *Hard Times*. In *Mary Barton* and *Ruth* (1853) Gaskell also gives a sympathetic account of the economic circumstances which lead to prostitution.

In the United States the major socio-political issue of the nineteenth century was not industrialization but slavery, and the single best-selling book of the whole century was Harriet Beecher Stowe's *Uncle Tom's Cabin* (1852), which roused sympathy for slaves and is widely credited with having played a major part in bringing about the abolition of slavery. This novel, like some of those written by nineteenth-century British women interested in social issues, was for a long time dismissed as being overly sentimental in its appeal, but more recently its literary qualitites have been re-evaluated. It is difficult to think of any single literary work written by a man which can be said to have had a similar political impact.

Another genre in which women were among the earliest and most successful practitioners is the Gothic novel, a form which flourished in the late eighteenth and early nineteenth centuries. Gothic novels usually place their central character – often but not always a woman – in a threatening and unfamiliar situation, often in an isolated place, confronting circumstances in which sinister forces, perhaps more than merely natural, may be at work. After their heyday Gothic novels were often dismissed as sensational and unrealistic, but they are now more commonly regarded as providing, in a pre-Freudian era, the exploration and dramatization of secret fears and emotions, perhaps of elements of the unconscious. The Gothic thus offers an alternative to the rational, factual and pragmatic world view which usually prevails and which also is usually associated with masculine values.

One of the most enduring, if not the most typical, of the Gothic novels is Mary Shelley's *Frankenstein* (1818). Its title character is a man who, withdrawing from normal life, is able through intense study and experiment to give life to a creature of his own making. Despite the success of his experiment, its results are ultimately disastrous. Mary Shelley is able to project recognizable human needs and feelings onto the 'monster' which Frankenstein creates; failing to measure up to his creator's standards, the monster is isolated and unloved, and in his frustration he becomes a destroyer.

The novel implicitly calls into question the positivistic and mechanistic world view associated with scientific and technological progress, which flourished in Mary Shelley's lifetime. The story insists on the human and emotional consequences which may accompany such advancement and undercut its apparent value. Mary Shelley also criticizes her character Frankenstein for abandoning personal relationships, especially those offered by his father and his sweetheart, in favour of his 'inhuman' scientific activities. Thus while *Frankenstein* has no central female character, it reflects values which, in its time, were more likely to be espoused by women than by men, and it implicitly calls into question values associated with a culture in which masculine values are dominant.

Much literature written by women, in whatever period, clearly reflects the contemporary social and political situation. Even in our own time, when many advances have been made, women are still not treated equally in many respects, and many values traditionally thought of as 'feminine' are exercised mainly in the private sphere and are not well reflected in public policy. Some feminist students of literature believe that literature written by women should not merely reflect or highlight this situation, but should actively seek to change it. 'Prescriptive' criticism, espoused by some (but by no means all) feminist critics, attempts to identify the ways in which literature can assist in this process of reform. Yet it is often difficult to see how realistic fiction with a contemporary setting (the dominant literary mode of our time) can also provide models of an improved cultural situation. While it may be desirable to create, for example, women characters who are strong and free, in the hope that these may serve as 'role models' for women readers, to do so may also seem to imply that ordinary women must develop heroic qualities in order to overcome enormous odds; our societies do not encourage women to be strong and free as yet. On the other hand, if literary works mainly emphasize the various difficulties and disabilities against which women must struggle, they may seem to present a hopeless picture and to ignore the real strengths and resources that women do, in fact, possess.

Some of these problems are avoided by writers working in other modes than that of realistic fiction. Many women, both in our own time and earlier, have written works of fantasy and science fiction which are relevant to their culture without directly reflecting it. Ursula K. Le Guin's *The Dispossessed* (1974), in which the central character is in fact male, contrasts two societies on different planets. One of these was created by a woman and provides equality, including sexual equality, but tends to stifle individual initiative. In the other, women are given no paid employment or public function and serve merely to provide sexual services for the men, who are nevertheless – if they are of the élite – encouraged to be intellectually active and productive. The novel is ultimately concerned with the need to integrate the best aspects of both these societies into one, and it does not underestimate the difficulties of doing so.

Utopian works, depicting a new and better world with different cultural values and a different social organization, have always provided a few writers with a means of suggesting alternatives to the existing arrangements. (The term *utopia* was first used by Thomas More in 1516, and is derived from the Greek *ou-topia*, meaning *no-place*.) Charlotte Perkins Gilman's *Herland* (1915) depicts – not without humour – a self-sufficient world of women into which a few bemused men stray; they emerge enlightened.

The obverse of a Utopia, sometimes called a *dystopia*, is a projection into the future of what may come about if certain current trends are not halted. Margaret Atwood's *The Handmaid's Tale* (1986) pictures a society in which only a few women are able to breed, and these are forced to do so at the command of a male ruling class.

Utopian and dystopian writings are by definition didactic, while much science fiction and other fantasy provides an alternative vision with a less clearly programmatic message. By departing from the world with which we are familiar, such works can help to free us from preconceptions about what is 'natural' or 'necessary' in our social arrangements, and perhaps help us to begin to conceive of new ones.

In attempting to indicate areas in which women have made distinctive or notable contributions to literature, we are of course focusing on themes, subjects or genres in which a number of women writers have made similar, or related, contributions. But it is by no means the case that all, or perhaps even most, women writers write about such topics as relations between women or social and moral issues. Nor have all, or even most, women writers throughout history consciously shared feminist political aims. The variety of work which has been produced by women writers is so great that it is impossible to summarize it, or fit it into a few convenient categories. Indeed, there is a danger that we may lose sight of certain women writers precisely because they are not 'typical' or 'representative'. In keeping an eye out for works by women, we should beware of assuming that, because women have certain distinctive experiences, their interests and talents are less varied than those of men. Likewise we should not assume that 'literature *by* women' is the same thing as 'literature mostly *for* women'.

Is women's writing feminist writing?

Generally we can say that feminism has two aspects. First, it identifies inequalities and injustices in the way girls and women are treated in a particular society, and the disabilities and disadvantages which result from these. A primary aim of feminism is to work to eliminate mistreatment and unequal treatment of women, at the same time understanding that the exact situation of women can differ enormously in different cultures and at different stages of history. The means used to bring about changes in the situation of women may include political action (to change laws, for example, or to increase the participation of women in political life); they may also include attempts to influence public opinion by calling attention to the actual situation of women and the need to improve it.

The second aspect of feminism is that it asserts the value, and the values, of women – the human dignity and worth of each individual woman and also the distinctive contributions that women make to their culture. It is in relation to this aspect of feminism that one may direct attention to previously under-valued accomplishments of women (in needlework, horticulture and folk medicine, for example). Here too one may find an emphasis on the social and cultural necessity of activities such as nurturing, caring for the helpless, and providing others with emotional support – activities generally carried out and valued highly by women. Likewise, feminism points to the forgotten or submerged contributions of women to fields apparently dominated by men. Literature is one of these latter.

Only a relatively small number of women writers have been consciously and explicitly feminist in the sense that they have identified 'the wrongs of women' (to use Mary Wollstonecraft's phrase) and deliberately worked to bring about social and political change, whether with the help of their literary work or by other means. We should however not lose sight of the fact that some of the most generally acclaimed women writers, including Elizabeth Barrett Browning and Virginia Woolf, were in fact 'feminist writers' in this explicit sense.

What is much more common, however, is to find that there is a rather less obvious feminist aspect to the work of a woman writer. In *Emma* (1814), Jane Austen does not explicitly comment on or reject a social and economic order which condemns unmarried women like Miss Bates and Jane Fairfax to a life of poverty or of dependence and probable loneliness. The only immediate remedy which Austen appears to propose for this situation is that better-off women should treat less-fortunate women with respect, kindness and generosity. For the reader, however, the novel may well have the effect of calling attention to the fundamental injustice of the situation, and in this respect the novel might well be said to have a feminist element.

As we have already seen with Virginia Woolf and Tillie Olsen, other works may highlight women's activities and help the reader to appreciate the importance and significance of aspects of life which might otherwise be passed over or dismissed as trivial. Literary works which do this bear a relationship to a feminist consciousness even when they do not appear to cry out against injustice or support a programme for change (although Olsen's *Yonnondio* is politically radical in more ways than one). One might even say that the mere fact of devoting one's energy to writing about women is an implicit acknowledgement of the value of women.

In any period however there are always some women who are consciously anti-feminist, either in the sense that they espouse the existing order wholeheartedly, or in the sense that they are generally unsympathetic to other women. Although Clare Boothe's play *The Women* is concerned only with women, the characters are almost uniformly presented as jealous, back-biting, scheming and resentful of one another. Most feminists would regard this picture as inconsistent with most women's actual experience of other women. Yet some feminist readers see Boothe's play as a condemnation of the social and economic pressures to which the characters are subjected; if security and status depend entirely upon one's ability to appeal to a well-off and powerful man, other women may appear principally as rivals for his attention.

A number of other women writers have made careers out of producing popular romances in which the essential plot involves an attractive but somewhat diffident young woman achieving marriage with a successful man; 'doctor and nurse' novels are a familiar version. Such works usually treat the emotional aspirations of the main character, and present her sense of self-doubt and insecurity, sympathetically. In one sense, by emphasizing the 'private' values of love and relationship, and by giving great attention to the internal emotional state of the main character, such works may seem to reflect women's values. On the other hand, by implying that the only source of satisfaction is romantic love, and the only hope of achieving economic security lies in marriage, such novels reinforce cultural presuppositions which in fact are very limiting and even directly damaging to women.

Thus we cannot assume a simple relationship between feminism and women's writing. Nevertheless it is natural to look to women's writing as at least potentially providing insights into women's lives and experiences which may be relevant for a feminist analysis. At worst, works written by and for women can help us to understand the force of prevailing stereotypes. And in particular, we can look to the writing of women in cultures other than our own to help us to an imaginative understanding of their situation – an understanding which is a necessary prerequisite to the ideal of an international 'sisterhood'.

Do women write differently from men?

In *A Room of One's Own*, Virginia Woolf observes that at the beginning of the nineteenth century there was a prevailing literary style based on what she calls 'a man's sentence . . . unsuited to a woman's use.' She adds, 'Jane Austen looked at it and laughed and devised a perfectly natural shapely sentence proper for her own use and never departed from it.[4] Woolf does not explain what she considers to be the distinguishing characteristics of 'the man's sentence', nor why it is unsuited for women writers, nor exactly how Jane Austen's sentence differs from it, and no later commentators on Woolf's work have produced a convincing elucidation of her ideas on this point. Furthermore, later in the same work Woolf, apparently contradicting herself, says 'It is fatal for anyone who writes to think of their sex. It is fatal to be a man or woman pure and simple; one must be woman-manly or man-womanly. It is fatal for a woman to lay the least stress on any grievance; to plead even with justice for any cause; in any way to speak consciously as a woman.'[5]

The issues raised here by Virginia Woolf have recurred. Is there anything distinctive in the way in which women write? Should there be?

Linguists have generally held that in languages which have been studied, there are some identifiable differences between the ways in which men and women talk – in such areas, for example, as vocabulary, intonation and subject matter as well as in less readily analysed features such as style of discourse and conventions of interaction between speakers (who is allowed to interrupt, for example). Although these assumptions and the evidence which is used to support them have been questioned of late, it still seems reasonable enough to ask whether there might be similar differences in the writing – especially the literary writing – of men and women.

Approaching the matter from a different perspective, some feminists hold that, as the public world is dominated by men, the language of public communication, including much literary communication, has been formed to suit men's needs – including the need to remain dominant over women. For women to adopt, or to continue to use, this masculine-orientated language and style of discourse is to do themselves a disservice, according to this view.

At the heart of this discussion is the question of the source of the differences which exist between women and men. Certainly one source of difference is biological *sex*, by virtue of which we are *male* and *female*. In addition, however, we know that cultures tend to divide many human characteristics and activities into two groups – to label some of these *masculine*, and regard them as appropriate for *men*, while others are labelled *feminine* and assigned to *women*. This opposition, based on culture rather than biology, is referred to as *gender*, and is distinguished from *sex*. We know that gender distinctions are not the same everywhere; they vary from culture to culture. We are born with sex, but we acquire gender – and there are always some individuals who do not completely adopt the gender characteristics which their society regards as appropriate to their sex.

It is often a matter of intense debate whether a particular observable difference between women and men is a necessary and essential one, a result of sex, or whether it is rather arbitrary and accidental, a result of gender differentiation.

The most concentrated theoretical discussion of these issues, as they relate particularly to literary language, has taken place amongst French theorists whose work is only now becoming widely known in the English-speaking world. These theorists are generally highly trained in the French philosophical tradition, and take as their starting point the work of the French psychoanalytic theorist, Jacques Lacan; people educated in the English-language traditions of psychology and literary theory often find the work of these French writers difficult and inaccessible, although greater efforts are now being made to become familiar with it.

A central question in the debate of these theorists is the relationship between psychology and language. Luce Irigaray, for example, believes that physical and therefore cognitive experiences differ considerably between the two sexes, and that one can expect these differences to be reflected in writing. The discourse of men, she believes, tends to be linear and to lead to definitive conclusions, while that of women, if left to develop freely, would be more wide-ranging and diffuse. Women have however been taught to alter this natural language (*le parler femme*, sometimes translated as *womanspeak*) for the purposes of discourse with men.

Another, but conflicting, possibility is that it is differences in nurture (the way one is raised) which create distinctive mental habits which are reflected in writing. In either case one might expect to find an *écriture féminine* (female, or feminine, writing) to use Hélène Cixous's phrase. (The French adjective *féminine* is the equivalent of both the English *female* and the English *feminine* and is therefore itself equivocal on the question of sex vs. gender.) However, Cixous herself in fact tends to think of literary writing as embodying both 'masculine' and 'feminine' characteristics, and offering all writers a means of escaping from the limiting categories of gender.

Some other theorists, including Julia Kristeva, believe that it is false to assume that there is only one, central opposition between 'masculine' and 'feminine' writing. While there may be one dominant mode of writing, based on reason, logic, linear development and chronology, there are in fact myriad other modes of writing which can serve as alternatives to this predominant mode. Even though men are usually attracted to the dominant mode (and logic and reason are assumed to be masculine), writers who use alternative modes may be either male or female. For example, both James Joyce and Dorothy Richardson pioneered the associative, anti-logical, non-chronological stream of consciousness form in fiction.

As this very brief summary indicates, there is no general agreement among literary theorists, including feminist ones, on the question of why men and women tend to write differently (if they do) and whether it is necessary, or might be desirable, for them to do so. The French discussion has furthermore taken place with very little reference to particular literary texts, although the theorists themselves often write in unconventional ways which may mirror their theoretical convictions. Literary theorists and critics in the English-speaking world are however becoming increasingly involved in this debate, and its scope is likely to widen further.

2 Why has Women's Writing been Undervalued?

Literature by women has been forgotten

In *A Room of One's Own*, Virginia Woolf gives an imaginative account of why a woman in the sixteenth century ('Shakespeare's sister') would find it virtually impossible to produce literature of lasting worth like her brother's. She lacked education and economic resources (to buy books and paper, for example) and she had little or no privacy or unsupervised free time. Among the few women writers of the nineteenth century who have long been held in high esteem – Jane Austen, Charlotte and Emily Brontë, George Eliot, Emily Dickinson – none had a child. Woolf's work emphasizes the obstacles which prevented women from writing. Tillie Olsen's *Silences* (1974) offers a more up-to-date elaboration of a similar idea.

Since the advent of the women's movement in the late 1960s in Western countries, women themselves have increasingly wanted to read, study and discuss literary works by other women, and have shared their own favourites and discoveries with others. One of the major results of the movement has been to call attention to the fact that women have, in fact, written a great deal more than even a widely-read person like Virginia Woolf would have realized in the 1920s. But much of this writing, including some which was widely esteemed in its own time, was quickly forgotten; it became generally unavailable and therefore did not, for example, become part of the reading usually required of students in schools, colleges and universities.

It has now been convincingly shown that a very high proportion of the early writers of novels (in the eighteenth and early nineteenth centuries) were women. At the same time the novel as a genre was initially not valued highly, and it took many years before novel-reading was regarded as a serious (or, in some cases, even as a respectable) activity. Furthermore, many of the women who wrote novels did so (like many of the men) with the deliberate intention of making money rather than creating 'works of art'. Yet although women constituted by far the greatest proportion of readers of novels, and a high proportion of writers of them, publishing and reviewing were, and are, overwhelmingly controlled by men.

Among the milestones of feminist literary scholarship are works which have attempted to broaden our view of the extent of women's literary activity, such as Ellen Moers's *Literary Women* (1976), which treats women (not all of them from English-speaking countries) who regarded writing as a profession. Elaine Showalter's *A Literature of Their Own* (1977, revised 1984) starts by recognizing that women and men have always tended to read somewhat different works. She observes that writers like Jane Austen and the Brontës may have shared a tradition of literature written by other women which was not widely known among men in their own generation and has been forgotten since. From a man's point of view, women writers therefore may seem to fall outside the main literary tradition.

As the novel established itself as a serious art form, increasing numbers of men wrote novels, and the genre attracted increasingly serious critical appreciation. Although certainly many men wrote about love and marriage – often as part of a larger plot – the tendency, noted previously, to consider 'men's subjects' serious and major, and 'women's subjects' trivial or minor, came into play. A notable number of nineteenth-century women novelists, including the Brontë sisters and 'George Eliot' (Mary Ann Evans) published first under masculine or equivocal pseudonyms, rightly believing that the ostensible sex of the author influenced critical reception of a work. It has, for example, been shown that evaluations of Emily Brontë's *Wuthering Heights* (1847) changed subtly but significantly when it became known that the author was a woman.[1]

We also know that women were explicitly discouraged from taking themselves seriously as writers. In Victorian times particularly there was much pressure on women to see to it that their literary careers did not interfere with their domestic responsibilities. Likewise it was considered unsuitable for women to treat certain subjects in their writing. Women's writing could thus be labelled improper as well as insignificant. And even if a particular writer or her work were granted esteem, she would be regarded as unusual, not as one of a large company of serious and notable writers, many of whom were women. Joanna Russ, herself a writer of science fiction, has summarized the obstacles faced by women in achieving lasting literary reputations in her witty but hard-hitting *How To Suppress Women's Writing* (1983).

These comments apply particularly to fiction, where women nevertheless have had the greatest success at establishing lasting reputations. The situation is even more difficult with regard to poetry and worst of all in respect of drama. Virginia Woolf believed that writing fiction, although scarcely easy, required less concentration (that is, less free time and privacy) than writing poetry or drama, and that this fact explained the relative paucity of women poets and dramatists. Most women poets from the sixteenth to the nineteenth centuries were either aristocratic or childless.

The writing of poetry was furthermore assumed, throughout this period, to take place against the background of an extensive education, notably in the classics. While a few aristocratic women had access to a form of classical education, it was rare for a middle-class woman to have an extensive literary education until the latter part of the nineteenth century. Women might, of course, write poetry on other premises, and a considerable number of them did, but such poetry was likely to be regarded as inferior *per se*, at best a 'popular' rather than an 'artistic' product. Individual poems published in periodicals were only occasionally included in collections or anthologies. Writing so treated, even today, is rarely preserved (in libraries, for example) in a readily accessible form, and it is therefore quickly forgotten.

Furthermore, the writing of verse is seldom lucrative, and the financial motivation which prompted many eighteenth- and nineteenth-century women to write fiction is largely absent in the case of poetry. Many women poets before the twentieth century either circulated their work privately or kept it entirely to themselves, and in many cases it is more or less a matter of accident if we are familiar with it at all. Emily Dickinson, who is now the most highly regarded women poet of the nineteenth century, published almost nothing during her own lifetime although she was an extremely productive poet.

Of the women poets who did publish and achieve popularity in their own lifetimes, many did so precisely because they confined themselves to topics and sentiments considered 'lady-like'; as a result much of this verse appeared to be conventional or sentimental, and regard for it did not persist beyond its own generation. Some of the more serious and adventuresome poets, such as Elizabeth Barrett Browning and Christina Rossetti, suffered a particularly ironic fate. Only those poems which were considered appropriately 'feminine' were frequently anthologized and therefore handed on to a future generation. Thus school children all over the English-speaking world have known Elizabeth Barrett Browning's love sonnets for generations, but her poems about political subjects or about artistic creation were ignored and virtually forgotten for over a century.

As for drama, women were prohibited from any association with the English theatre until the end of the seventeenth century; the few women's roles in plays such as those by Shakespeare were performed by boys. Thereafter, even up to fairly recent times, such women as were associated with the theatre were regarded as morally dubious, and it required considerable indifference to public opinion for a woman like Aphra Behn to persist in writing plays and to treat 'racy' subjects.

Even today, only a tiny number of women write plays which achieve professional production. Only a small proportion of plays (whatever the sex of the writer) are notably successful, and in general only plays which have been successful, or have been written by very well-established playwrights, are likely to be published. Publication itself is the usual prerequisite to a play's continued life and production in the theatre; it is certainly essential if the play is to become widely known and used, for example, as part of educational courses, although the recent proliferation of video equipment provides an alternative means of recording and circulating dramatic works. As women are so little represented among professional dramatists in any case, the number whose work survives all these sifting processes is miniscule indeed.

Michelene Wandor speculates that, at another level, the reason why so few women succeed as dramatists is that drama, unlike poetry or the novel, is essentially a public art, and our culture has not generally encouraged women to have a public role or a public voice.[2] Certainly it is notable that, although actresses have the same public status as actors, there are far fewer roles for women in the standard repertoire, and while there are many leading roles for men of about forty or fifty years of age, most such roles for women are for *young* women. This situation reflects the general tendency of our culture to regard women as interesting mainly while they are potentially fertile; opening the theatre to more women dramatists would no doubt produce more plays about women at all stages of their lives.

In general one may conclude that much writing by women is implicitly regarded as being of limited value precisely because it is about women and may appeal mainly or especially to women readers, who are regarded as a 'special' rather than as a general or typical audience. Even writing by women which does not readily fall into this category is likely to be treated as if it did. It is commonplace, for example, for a number of works by women to be grouped together for review in a newspaper or literary magazine, and for women reviewers (who are in a distinct minority) to be steered toward reviewing works by women. This custom reinforces the tendency to assume that work by women, whatever its content, and however much it is praised, somehow does not belong to the 'mainstream'.

Non-literary writing

Although, as we have seen, there have been various constraints against women writing and publishing poetry, fiction and drama, we are now aware that much of women's creative and literary energy has gone into other forms of writing than these traditionally enumerated genres. Much writing by women is not initially intended for public consumption. Letters, diaries and journals written by women often provide fascinating insights into women's lives, emotions and opinions. Some of these, such as the fifteenth-century Paston letters (some of which were written by women) furnish social and economic historians with unique sources of information about domestic arrangements, estate management and the interaction of various social groups and classes. Others, like the letters of the seventeenth-century French aristocrat, Mme de

Sévigné, give invaluable information about what went on behind the scenes in political life at the same time as they serve as a monument to the writer's impassioned love for her daughter. Such 'non-literary' writings can at times elicit from women works which, in terms of observation of character, insight, style and expression of emotion, are comparable to fiction or poetry.

Another category of writing by women which has recently received renewed attention is devotional and theological writing. Some of this writing tends to be concentrated in certain periods and certain religious groups – many nonconformist women wrote theological works in the nineteenth century, for example.

Women are also more heavily represented among mystical writers than men are. From the Middle Ages, there has been a strong and frequently-noted tendency for mystical writers of either sex to use erotic imagery to describe the relation of the soul to God. If God is conventionally thought of as masculine, perhaps women like the sixteenth-century Spanish nun, Teresa of Avila, have an advantage in writing about a spiritual union with 'him', developing a convention in which nuns are referred to as the 'brides of Christ'. Conversely, the most famous of the English mystical writers, the fourteenth-century anchoress, Julian of Norwich, in one of her works imagines God as a mother because of the loving care with which God attends the soul.

Mystical writing is by no means an exclusively medieval phenomenon, nor is it exclusively Christian. The mystical strain can be found in the work of writers as recent as the mid twentieth-century English Catholic Caryll Houselander and the French Jew Simone Weil. The American Mary Daly, originally trained as a theologian, now writes difficult-to-classify works, such as her *Gyn/Ecology* (1978), with elements of theology, philosophy, poetry and polemic.

Material by women which does not fall into the traditional categories of fiction, poetry and drama has frequently been excluded from academic consideration on the grounds that it is not 'really literature'. At the same time, texts by men, such as John Donne's sermons, John Milton's essays, the autobiography of Benjamin Franklin and James Boswell's life of Samuel Johnson are included with few or no apologies. Academic courses and recent anthologies devoted to women's writing are now tending to break down such barriers and enlarge our conception of the kinds of writing which may merit our attention.

Re-evaluating the 'canon'

In talking about 'English literature', and more especially in arranging courses of study in literature, there is usually a silent assumption that we know, at least roughly speaking, who the important writers are and what texts are representative of major developments in literary history. These writers and texts constitute what is often referred to as 'the canon' – that is, the essential core of an entity which we call 'English literature'. Writers and texts to be taught and assigned are selected from among these.

There is an implicit assumption that 'the best' or 'the greatest' writers and texts are ones which survive their own time and that, with some help from education, almost any intelligent reader can recognize which these are. Agreement among scholars and critics about the values of these writers and texts is thought to be a natural result of their inherent excellence, although in fact readers – even professional ones – often find it hard to define just exactly what qualities make a text 'good' or 'great'.

Even a fairly cursory study of the reception given to literary works, and of the changing 'reputations' of writers will, however, bring into question the idea that 'English literature' is a stable phenomenon and that the value of major texts and writers is more or less self-evident. Shakespeare himself, now long thought of as 'the greatest writer the world has ever known', was regarded as of dubious merit in the late seventeenth and early eighteenth centuries. A number of seventeenth-century poets, often collectively referred to as 'the Metaphysicals', were regarded as distinctly minor until the poet and critic T. S. Eliot resurrected them, almost single-handedly, in the middle of the present century. There are, conversely, many examples of writers whose work was regarded with suspicion, or rejected, in their own time but who have been viewed with much greater favour by later generations. And, although scholars and critics are usually much more cautious about assigning permanent high status to living writers, an examination of major literary awards such as the Nobel Prize will reveal that a number of recipients have been all but forgotten in later generations even though others continue to be highly regarded.

All of these circumstances tend to call into question the idea that literary merit is self-evident and lasting and that it is obvious which works and writers constitute a 'canon' which should be passed on to future generations through academic programmes.

In recent years feminist critics and those interested in literature by other minority groups (such as colonial and Commonwealth writers, blacks, indigenous peoples and homosexuals) have argued that the prevailing notion of what 'English literature' consists of, and what texts are central, is in fact determined, not by 'universal' or 'lasting' criteria, but by the values of the most powerful group in our society, middle- and upper-class white men. In order to reach this conclusion, one does not need to assume that individual literary critics and scholars who come from this group have deliberately and maliciously suppressed most of the literary work of other groups. Rather, it would be natural enough if members of this group in general respond to, prefer and hand on literary works which reflect and authenticate their own experiences and values. But the result is the same – works written by and for this group will make up a very large proportion of the 'canon'.

It is historically typical that groups which are asserting, or attempting to gain, increased political power will resurrect and re-examine cultural phenomena and achievements of their own group in earlier times, and will encourage members of their own group to make distinctive cultural contributions. This activity helps members of marginalized social groups to establish a sense of identity and significance. For example, the movement often known as the Irish Literary Revival arose in connection with Irish political nationalism around the turn of the century. And, if such groups succeed in achieving greater political power or become more integrated into the culture which surrounds them, their achievements, including rediscovered achievements, will generally become accepted as part of the larger culture. Thus W. B. Yeats and James Joyce are now accepted as having an assured place in 'English literature'.

Feminist literary critics argue that many ignored or forgotten texts by women are at least as valuable as many of the texts, written by men, now regarded as standard. Scholarly studies of publishing history have shown that, in general, works by women are more likely to go out of print than works by men; they are therefore less likely to be read and handed on by future generations of readers and teachers. This state of affairs is certainly related to the fact that publishing, criticism and the academy are still principally male domains, although this situation has changed somewhat in recent years.

As we have 'seen, much scholarship has been devoted to resurrecting and re-evaluating 'lost' or 'forgotten' works by women; while no one would claim that every such lost work deserves to be widely read, in many cases literary reputations have been significantly altered. Perhaps the most notable case is that of the American Kate Chopin, previously remembered largely as a writer of 'regional' short stories. Her novel *The Awakening* (1899) was initially suppressed, largely because its subject matter was thought shocking; it was reprinted for the first time in the 1960s and is now widely thought of as her masterpiece; its resurrection has increased her stature significantly.

A number of publishing houses in the various English-speaking countries now specialize in, or confine themselves to, works by and about women. While these also provide an outlet for new works by women writers, several of them have concentrated on making rediscovered and re-evaluated work widely available again. These circumstances have produced what may fairly be called a revolution in the reading of literature written by women, and one effect is to make possible radical changes in literature teaching programmes in academic institutions.

The problem with such changes is, of course, that if more works by women (or by members of any of a number of other minority groups) are to be included in school, college and university syllabuses, something from the existing syllabus must give way for them, and this will usually mean the elimination or down-playing of work by men.

Feminist critics and teachers do not generally get involved in detailed arguments about exactly which male writers or works should be dislodged to give place for women writers. Their emphasis rather is usually on ensuring the inclusion of women in general courses, or providing special courses which concentrate on writing by women, and allowing students to select these from among several options. However, feminist criticism of works by male writers has sometimes demonstrated that women find certain works less valuable than men traditionally have done.

The earliest studies in the recent phase of feminist literary criticism (from about the end of the 1960s) in fact often concentrated, not on women writers, but on the way in which women were portrayed in literary works, especially those written by men. This approach, now referred to as 'Images of Women criticism', established very quickly that many male writers tended to create women characters who essentially were little more than stereotypes, or were defined almost exclusively in terms of their relationships (especially sexual relationships) with men. Sir Walter Scott's *Ivanhoe* (1819), for example, presents two women: the blonde, noble and pure Rowena and the dark, exotic, presumably passionate Rebecca. Such 'lily and rose' combinations are to be found not only in romantic literature, but also in more realistic works, as potential rivals for the male hero, who almost invariably chooses the blonde for his bride.

Similarly, as we have noted, in *Sexual Politics* Kate Millett demonstrates at some length that certain works by D. H. Lawrence (and also by less highly regarded writers such as Henry Miller and Normal Mailer) distort women's sexual and emotional responses and, in doing so, falsify the nature of women and of the relations between the sexes.

Scholars and critics who point out such features in the work of male writers do not necessarily draw the explicit conclusion that these writers are therefore without value. Nevertheless, to point out that a writer presents characters who seem stereotyped, limited or distorted in works which otherwise have been regarded as offering a high degree of insight into human experience, may in some cases call into question the stature of the work or the writer involved.

Feminist critics are not agreed about whether the 'canon' can be adjusted satisfactorily by the inclusion of more women writers. Some believe, more radically, that the idea of an agreed-upon body of English literature must be scrapped altogether although it is not clear what, if anything, should take its place. Feminist scholars and critics do however share the conviction that, in considering literature and literary history, one cannot look at a work in isolation and arrive at an 'objective' judgement about it. We never in fact look at anything absolutely objectively; our responses are partly conditioned by our education, our preconceptions and assumptions. One must also look at the circumstances of literary composition, the frame of mind of those who receive, evaluate and pass literature on, and at the responses of groups other than the most powerful if one is to make an informed judgement about the potential significance of a literary work.

3 Poetry

Our knowledge of women as poets goes back to classical anti-
quity; in the seventh century BC the Greek poet Sappho, born on
the island of Lesbos, wrote of love – and perhaps of other subjects as well, but we have only twelve of her poems to judge by,
and even these are incomplete. Myth and legend associated
with her name suggest that she was disappointed in love of a
man, left her home and thereafter concentrated her affections
on women companions; it is from her birthplace and residence
on Lesbos that our word 'lesbian' is derived. Whatever the truth
behind these dubious assumptions (for there is evidence that
politics rather than love led to Sappho's retreat from Lesbos),
she is still thought of as a lyric poet of great power. If our picture
of her as a love poet is one-sided, she is only the first of many
women poets of whom this is true.

Virginia Woolf, in *A Room of One's Own*, makes the
tantalizing suggestion that women may frequently have been
the anonymous composers of the folk ballads of the Middle
Ages, many of which are narrated from a woman's point of view
or have women as the principal figures. As for women poets
whose names we know, as we have already seen, it is striking
that, before the late eighteenth century, virtually all came from
aristocratic backgrounds. In England, for example, Queen
Elizabeth I wrote competent and attractive poems in English
and also translated from Latin. But she was exceptional in
having been accorded an education; even among aristocratic
women, many whose brothers were educated, were themselves illiterate.

Between the sixteenth and the eighteenth centuries there
were nevertheless some women in Britain who enjoyed high
literary reputations during their own lifetimes, but whose work

either was not preserved or was virtually forgotten by later generations. Among these was, for example, Lady Mary Sidney Herbert, the Countess of Pembroke (1561–1621), who is now remembered chiefly as the sister of Sir Philip Sidney but was greatly admired by her contemporaries. Having a well-educated and sympathetic brother (or husband) provided some women with the opportunity to achieve learning, and the encouragement to make use of it.

It is typical of these aristocratic literary women that they engaged in a variety of literary projects and used many forms, so that it is somewhat misleading to consider them only as poets; Mary Sidney Herbert, for example, translated plays, poems and prose works from various languages into English. She also took over work left incomplete at the time of her brother's death, completing a translation of the Psalms he had left unfinished. This work shows a mastery of a wide variety of poetic forms and the results deserve to be called independent poems rather than mere translations. Possibly one reason for the decline of Mary Sidney Herbert's reputation lies in the fact that, of her own work, only these translations of the Psalms survive.

Ironically, the fact that Mary Sidney Herbert was aristocratic was in itself a factor which would have worked against the ultimate preservation of her writings. The aristocratic male writers of her generation wrote primarily for circulation among their friends and at court; publication was a secondary and often rather incidental event. In any case publication of works by a woman would have seemed potentially improper; a much more relaxed attitude prevailed in the case of writings by men.

Much, although not all, of Mary Sidney Herbert's surviving work has religious subject matter, and this is a common element in much of the women's writing we know before the eighteenth century, whether in poetry or in other genres. Apart from the classical learning and education in languages which a fortunate aristocratic woman might receive, in the Middle Ages convents provided the only other significant source of literacy or learning for women and, as we have seen earlier, these religious institutions gave homes to mystical and devotional writers. The role of convents and monasteries as centres of learning was gradually effaced by the growing role of the universities in Europe generally during the late Middle Ages and the Renaissance, while in Britain the Reformation abolished these institutions, which never again attained more than a marginal role in the education of women.

Yet by the seventeenth century various nonconformist groups, acknowledging at least theoretically the spiritual equality of women and men, provided a context in which women wrote devotional and theological works, including poetry. Among these was Anne Bradstreet (1612–1672), one of the first poets of the New England colonies. Before leaving England, Bradstreet had evidently acquired considerable learning through private teaching and access to the library of the Earl of Lincoln, and this erudition is also reflected in her poetry. Thus not all of Bradstreet's work has a religious theme as its ostensible starting point, but, living as she did in a society whose whole *raison d'être* was religious, her faith informs virtually all of her judgements and interpretations. Thus, for example, she comforts herself in 'Some Verses upon the Burning of Our House, July 10, 1666: Copied out of a Loose Paper':

Then straight I 'gin my heart to chide,
And did thy wealth on earth abide?
Didst fix thy hope on mouldering dust?
The arm of flesh didst make thy trust?
Raise up thy thoughts above the sky
That dunghill mists away may fly.
Thou hast a house on high erect,
Framed by that mighty Architect.

That in the circumstances of sudden homelessness she apparently located a piece of paper and began to write, says much about the force of Bradstreet's creative drive. This poem, combining original imagery with orthodox Puritan concepts and language, gives a good sense of the flavour of her work. Her poems, brought out in England without her knowledge or consent, constituted the first published volume of verse from the American colonies; they became very popular, and Bradstreet's reputation has remained high ever since.

The number of literary women whom we know of increases significantly as we move through the seventeenth century and toward the eighteenth, but women from aristocratic backgrounds continue to predominate, especially among the poets, while their subject matter is increasingly more likely to be secular than was the case previously. One seventeenth-century poet who is often thought of as a forerunner of eighteenth-century writers is Katherine Philips (1631–64). Philips came from a Puritan background but developed Royalist sympathies which she expressed in her poetry, a proceeding which must have required no small degree of courage. As part of a literary and intellectual group which included her husband, Katherine Philips adopted a pseudo-classical pen-name, and was long referred to as 'The Matchless Orinda', an epithet which gives some evidence of the regard her contemporaries had for her and her work. In addition to being respected for her poetry (although it was not published during her lifetime) she produced translations of Corneille which were performed in London with great success.

Although Philips seems to have been content in her marriage, the subject which appears to have given her the strongest promptings toward poetry was her friendship with another member of her circle, a woman whom she addresses as 'Lucasia', and for whom she sometimes expresses love framed in romantic terms which invite us to consider her as writing in the tradition of Sappho.

No bridegroom's or crown-conqueror's mirth
To mine compared can be:
They have but pieces of this earth;
I've all the world in thee.

> (From 'To My Excellent Lucasia, On Our Friendship')

Philips's poems addressed to 'Lucasia' are historically notable but some modern readers may find their appeal limited, their originality lying more in choice of subject matter than in expression; some feel that Philips's Royalist poems, such as 'Upon the Double Murther of King Charles I', are more individual in expression and correspondingly convey more passion.

By the latter part of the seventeenth century, Aphra Behn (1640–89) had appeared on the scene; the author of plays, poems and a novel, *Oronooko* (1688), sometimes called the first novel in English, Behn is frequently described as the first professional woman of letters in England. Of middle-class origins, and evidently possessing an adventurous disposition, she lacked some of the scruples which had hitherto discouraged aristocratic women from publishing. Finding herself financially unprovided for, Aphra Behn wrote with the aim of making a living. In consequence, she was often regarded as a scandalous figure, not least by other, more discreet women writers. Behn's willingness to write poetry which was as explicit sexually as that of some of the men who wrote toward the end of the seventeenth century, did nothing to make her appear more respectable, but she seems to have been quite undisturbed by the reputation she acquired.

A rather younger contemporary of Aphra Behn's is Anne Finch, Duchess of Winchilsea (1661–1720), who can most readily be seen as a successor of Katherine Philips. A considerably more prolific poet, she also occasionally wrote on female friendship, used 'classical' pseudonyms and, like Philips earlier, wrote verse which suggested that she was fortunate in a happy marriage and a husband who did not discourage her writing. Her two verse dramas were seen in their own time as being plainly derivative from those of Philips.

Finch lived in some retirement but nevertheless was known and respected in literary circles in her own time; she was friendly with both Alexander Pope and Jonathan Swift. For later generations, she was particularly notable as having written some of the earliest eighteenth-century poetry on nature, pointing to what was to become the central subject for Romantic poetry of the later eighteenth and earlier nineteenth centuries. Her contribution to this development was recognized and praised by William Wordsworth.

Finch appears to have suffered from bouts of what we would now call depression; in 'The Spleen' (i.e. melancholy), she offers a heartfelt account of the various forms this emotional misery can take. Not least, she includes the possibility that women like herself are frustrated by being expected to engage in conventional 'artistic' pursuits instead of following their authentic creative impulses:

Whilst in the Muses's path I stray,
Whilst in their groves, and by their secret springs
My hand delights to trace unusual things,
And deviates from the known, and common way;
Nor will in fading silks compose
Faintly th' inimitable rose,
Fill up an ill-drawn bird, or paint on glass
The sovereign's blurred and undistinguished face.

Anne Finch published only one volume of poems during her lifetime. By the end of the eighteenth century, however, many of the forces which had tended to discourage women from publishing had dissipated, and the professional woman of letters became a real, if not widespread, phenomenon. Literacy spread, and schools providing a form of education for girls (although a very limited one) had begun to appear. The writing woman ceased to be primarily an aristocratic phenomenon and became a largely middle-class one.

Prosperity and a degree of leisure nevertheless continued to be of major importance for women poets. Of the three most respected women poets who wrote in English during the nineteenth century, two, Emily Dickinson and Christina Rossetti, never married, while the third, Elizabeth Barrett Browning, had established her reputation before she met her very sympathetic and supportive husband, the poet Robert Browning.

Elizabeth Barrett Browning (1806–61) was so much admired in her own day that she was regarded as a potential Poet Laureate, but in later generations she was remembered only for one or two of her *Sonnets from the Portuguese* (1850), addressed to her husband; the romantic story of their courtship and marriage eclipsed Barrett Browning's own literary accomplishments, although it never took precedence in accounts of her husband's career.

Although her love poems are certainly worth remembering, Elizabeth Barrett Browning was a woman engaged on many fronts, not least politics, and a wide variety of concerns are reflected in her poetry. Amongst other things she wrote about the nature of poetry and of poetic inspiration. She was a prolific writer, and she employed a considerable variety of poetic forms. She was furthermore anything but provincial; living the latter part of her life in Italy, she was much absorbed by the Italian nationalist movement, about which she wrote extensively in *Casa Guidi Windows* (1851) and *Poems before Congress* (1860).

Some of her most striking and memorable poems take up other issues of her time; 'The Runaway Slave at Pilgrim's Point' is a monologue spoken by a black American slave woman who has been raped by her master, borne a child, killed it because it constantly reminded her of white supremacy, and then been flogged in punishment. The speaker contrasts the American

The works of women are symbolical.
We sew, sew, prick our fingers, dull our sight,
Producing what? A pair of slippers, sir,
To put on when you're weary – or a stool
To stumble over and vex you . . . 'curse that stool!'
. . . .
This hurts most, this – that, after all, we are paid
The worth of our work, perhaps.
                    (Book One)

After many vicissitudes, including Romney's failed attempts
to marry a woman he had assumed he could shape to his own
wishes, Aurora and Romney are finally united, but only after he
is blinded and therefore made entirely dependent upon her. In
the end, she is thus permitted to achieve love, the value of her
art is acknowledged, and she is encouraged to engage in significant public activity. Having been prepared to pay the price
demanded by her standards, Aurora is at last able to 'have it all',
as Elizabeth Barrett Browning herself had at length managed to
do, escaping at a mature age from the domination of a patho-
logically possessive father into her marriage with Robert
Browning, who fell in love with her, initially, because he
admired her poems.

The move involved courage, a potentially scandalous
elopement, and a life of exile, but rewarded the risk-takers. In
one of the *Sonnets from the Portuguese*, Barrett Browning
provides an initial image of two lovers as equals, passionate and
transcendent.

When our two souls stand up erect and strong
Face to face, silent, drawing nigh and nigher,
Until the lengthening wings break into fire
At either curved point, – what bitter wrong
Can earth do to us?

Aurora Leigh is not however only, or even mainly, concerned
with love between man and woman. Aurora befriends the bride
Romney never married when she has been deceived and
betrayed, and at the end, is approached by the noblewoman who
has schemed, unsuccessfully, to marry Romney herself. The
possibility of a sisterhood extending from the top to the bottom
of society's ranks is thus alluded to, although not explored fully.

Aurora Leigh, like most of the long poems the Victorians were so fond of, is not without its flaws, yet it did not deserve the obscurity to which it was so long consigned. Aurora's name means, literally, 'dawn', an association sometimes strengthened by the poem's imagery. In Barrett Browning's aspirations, she represents a 'new dawn' for women and for society; ironically, Aurora and what she stood for were too long eclipsed.

By contrast with Elizabeth Barrett Browning, the American poet Emily Dickinson (1830–86) lived obscurely and her work was virtually unknown during her lifetime; after her death, however, it was extensively published and acclaimed, and her reputation has never since diminished. If Elizabeth Barrett Browning's achievements have been obscured by the romance associated with her elopement and marriage, a contrasting, but equally sentimental, image of Emily Dickinson prevailed and tended to confuse accounts of her work, however much it was admired. She was long described as a recluse who withdrew from society and devoted herself to her poetry because of a hopeless love for a man about whose identity there was endless speculation. She was described as an eccentric, always dressing in white, never appearing in daylight, 'a New England nun'. Later and more scholarly investigation of her life has revealed that the extent of her seclusion has been much exaggerated, and that, far from having spent a lonely spinsterhood pining for a lost love, she kept a devoted admirer at a certain distance, evidently sharing his feelings but preferring to maintain a degree of solitude necessary for artistic concentration.

Dickinson was extremely productive, producing over 1700 poems, most of which were found in a variety of versions after her death. All of them are relatively short, many no more than eight or twelve lines long; they do not have titles. The physical appearance of these apparently 'little' poems, usually with stanzas of four short lines, contributed to the prevailing impression that Dickinson wrote dainty, maidenly works; on a page they looked very like nursery rhymes. Dickinson's first editors furthermore tidied up her verse to give it a more conventional appearance; they sometimes regularized her metres and chose versions with the most regular rhymes for publication.

In fact, Dickinson wrote verse highly unconventional for its time, and preferred not to publish rather than to alter her ways. Her notions of punctuation and capitalization were individual, and no completely satisfactory explanation of them has ever been given. She altered standard English grammar freely, creating new verb tenses and pushing existing words into new grammatical functions. Although most of her poems are based on the four-line ballad stanza which prevailed in the hymns she would have heard in church (before she decided to stop attending), she treats these metres very freely, shifting stress and employing many half-rhymes or using consonance in place of rhyme.

Dickinson was a contemporary of two other major innovators in poetic form, her fellow American Walt Whitman and the English Jesuit Gerard Manley Hopkins. Although aware of literary developments in her own time, she was, like Whitman and Hopkins, an entirely independent artist, a pathfinder.

Dickinson did for some time share with Barrett Browning the fate of having some of her least characteristic work most widely anthologized; a few relatively undemanding poems about birds, trains heard at a distance and lost love were taken to stand for the whole of her achievement. She is in fact a poet whose work should be read extensively if one is to get a sense of the breadth and depth of her achievement.

Many of her poems certainly appear to be about love, or at any rate about loss; many are about death – sometimes the speaker imagines her way into her own death, often she responds to the death of another. Many poems are addressed to God and, without being conventionally devout, the poet explores the possibilities of the relationship between the human and something beyond it. In general she gives a sense of writing about extremes, pushing experience as far as it will go and then attempting to imagine a survival and a consciousness beyond that point. The result is frequently a metaphysical speculation concentrated into a few lines of verse. In the following very complex stanzas, for example, she explores the problem of attempting to achieve internal harmony in a self in conflict.

Me from Myself – to banish –
Had I Art –
Impregnable my Fortress
Unto All Heart –

But since Myself – assault Me –
How have I peace

Except by subjugating
Consciousness?

And since We're mutual Monarch
How this be
Except by Abdication –
Me – of Me?

One may be tempted to consider that the poem is about trying to
persuade oneself to forget an unhappy love affair; but the text
gives no indication that its subject is so specific; internal division
and the integrity of the self are its themes.

Specifically feminist readings of Dickinson's work have not
been common, but Cora Kaplan has emphasized that Dickinson
knew and admired the work of Elizabeth Barrett Browning, and
has shown how both poets resisted the limits which convention
imposed upon women's artistic expression.[1]

They shut me up in Prose –
As when a little Girl
They put me in the Closet –
Because they liked me "still" –

Still! Could themself have peeped
And seen my Brain – go round –
They might as well have lodged a Bird
For Treason – in the Pound –

Himself has but to will
And easy as a Star
Abolish his Captivity
And laugh – No more have I –

Modern scholarship has treated Dickinson's work with the
respect it deserves.

Whereas the earliest sonnet sequences (first in Italian, then
French, coming into English in the sixteenth century) explored
love – and usually frustrated love – from a man's point of
view, Elizabeth Barrett Browning appropriated the genre to
female use. In this she was followed by the American poet Edna
St Vincent Millay (1892–1950), a writer who combined learning

and an intense consciousness of literary tradition with a clear, modern declarative style. Coming to public attention early in the 1920s, Millay cut a conspicuous figure in the Bohemian atmosphere of Greenwich Village, and was for some time thought of as a kind of female laureate of free love. This impression of her, and the linguistic accessibility of her work in the generation dominated by such abstruse poets as T. S. Eliot, made her popular to a degree that later generations regarded with some suspicion. Ten years after her death she had begun to slide into obscurity, but her work is now being taken seriously once again.

Millay certainly wrote poetry about love; occasionally it is specified as adulterous. By her own account she wrote in the tradition of Catullus and Baudelaire, and she is entirely unselfconscious about being a woman in their company. Her sonnet sequence *Fatal Interview* (1931), about a love affair whose failure can be predicted from the start, is explicit about the fact that women experience, and follow, sexual desires which may ill accord with their judgement. In this, of course, women are only human.

This beast that rends me in the sight of all,
This love, this longing, this oblivious thing,
That has me under as the last leaves fall,
Will glut, will sicken, will be gone by spring.   (ii)

Her treatment of this subject matter seems to connect her, initially, with Aphra Behn; certainly there has not been a serious woman poet in the interval whose work is so explicitly sexual. Yet Millay's treatment is rarely as light-hearted as that of Behn. Rather, her poems tend to relate modern experience to the past of legend, myth and history:

I only in such utter, ancient way
Do suffer love; in me alone survive
The unregenerate passions of a day
When treacherous queens, with death upon the tread,
Heedless and wilful, took their knights to bed.   (xxvi)

The sonnet was a favourite form, and love a favourite subject, but Millay's work, like that of Barrett Browning, was far more varied in both form and subject than her reputation indicates.

She was as much at home with free verse as with the sonnet and other strict forms and she wrote a number of ballads influenced by the folk tradition. She has poems about childhood, about art, death, religious belief and the lack of it. A considerable proportion of her poems were occasioned by public events and written in the public manner. She espoused a variety of liberal causes and wrote, for example, about the execution of Sacco and Vanzetti, the Spanish Civil War, the suffering of Czechoslovakia. In the pre-nuclear age she produced a sonnet sequence called *Epitaph for the Race of Man* (1934). She had an almost professional knowledge of botany and ornithology which appears in several of her poems, and she wrote frequently and vividly about animals.

And cats die. They lie on the floor and lash their tails,
And their reticent fur is suddenly all in motion
With fleas that one never knew were there,
Polished and brown, knowing all there is to know,
Trekking off into the living world.
You fetch a shoe-box, but it's much too small, because she
  won't curl up now:
So you find a bigger box, and bury her in the yard, and
  weep.

('Childhood is the Kingdom Where Nobody Dies')

Millay grew up in an all-female family, and her relationship with her mother and her two sisters was enviably warm and intimate, a constant anchor-point in her life. She was educated at two excellent women's colleges, Barnard and Vassar, and her attitudes were consciously feminist, although this fact perhaps emerges more clearly from her splendid, articulate letters than from her poems. Not least among her subjects is friendship, especially although not only with women, and at times she alludes to the tradition of Sappho. Some of her elegies for dead friends are especially memorable:

Let them bury your big eyes
In the secret earth securely,
Your thin fingers, and your fair,
Soft, indefinite coloured hair, –
. . .
Not for these I sit and stare,

Broken and bereft completely:
Your young flesh that sat so neatly
On your little bones will sweetly
Blossom in the air.
            ('Elegy')

With a poetic practice looking both forward and backward, with a combination of public and private themes and a distinctive but varied poetic voice, Millay is in fact one of the most representative poets of her time.

If Millay's reputation went into decline in the decades after her death, the reputation of another New-England-born poet, Sylvia Plath, has continued to rise since her suicide in 1963 at the age of thirty-one. Millay takes up public issues of her time in her poetry; Plath's, by contrast, is often so intensely inward-looking as to be almost oblivious of an objective external world, but it was early felt that she could be seen as a kind of representative of the ills of her generation – especially of its women.

Certainly her novel, *The Bell Jar*, provides a catalogue of the conflicting, destructive pressures which might be experienced by an intelligent, ambitious young woman in the 1950s. It was an era which provided women with education and professional training but insisted that their true fulfilment lay in marriage and motherhood, which stressed the importance of virginity but allowed quite free contact between the sexes and dwelt incessantly upon sexuality in its commercial culture.

In her poetry, however, Plath concentrates less on social pressures than on her own psychic history, with the death of her father when she was eight years old as a pivot. Her consequent sense of abandonment and continued helpless dependence is expressed by imaging him as a quintessential oppressor. Her most famous poem, 'Daddy', associates her German-speaking father with Hitler, and in other poems she compares herself to the victims of the Holocaust, although the point of the comparison seems to be that the historical tyranny mirrors her own private agony, rather than the other way around. The chiming of one rhyming sound (*do, you, shoe, Jew, screw*) throughout 'Daddy' suggests both obsession and the babbling of a child. For some readers, the relationship between the dependent female speaker and the oppressive father is a crystallization of the psychological situation of women in a patriarchal society.

In 'Daddy', the speaker struggles to release herself from

the grip of the memory of her father, trying even the self-annihilation of suicide as a means of escape. Plath did in fact make a famous suicide attempt several years before the final successful one, and was hospitalized and given various forms of psychiatric treatment, including electro-shock; these experiences appear in various forms in a number of her best known poems. In 'Lady Lazarus', whose title refers to the biblical character who rose from death, she begins 'I have done it again/ One year in every ten/ I manage it – ' and later continues 'Dying/Is an art, like everything else/ I do it exceptionally well./ I do it so it feels like hell'. The conclusion of 'Daddy' asserts that the speaker has gained her psychological freedom ('Daddy, Daddy, you bastard, I'm through') although in the light of Plath's later history readers often have difficulty in regarding this proclaimed release as more than merely rhetorical.

As these observations will suggest, a problem with reading Plath's work is that it often cannot be understood without reference to her life, and what is known about that often makes it difficult for the reader to respond to the poems spontaneously. Plath's self-absorption was such as to make her appear an unattractive character, in the view of some readers. On the other hand, the circumstances of her suicide, shortly after the break-up of her marriage to the poet Ted Hughes, have led other readers to sympathize with her to the extent, in effect, of blaming her husband for her death and, implicitly, the blighting of her career. She has at times been described as subsuming her own talent in that of her husband, obeying ancient cultural commands to women that they must take second place. Much of the evidence seems rather to suggest that coming together with Hughes was a crucial turning-point in Plath's artistic development and, despite the regrettable outcome, the last few months of her life were by far her most productive poetically.

Plath wrote several poems about motherhood, providing a notably unsentimental treatment of the subject and conveying the sense of ambivalence which is a common experience of women in a culture which gives lip-service to the idea of motherhood but in practical and economic terms makes life difficult for women who are responsible for the care of small children. 'Morning Song' conveys both a mother's wonder and pleasure in her baby's crowing, ('You try your handful of notes/The clear vowels rise like balloons') and her sense of being de-sexualized by childbirth ('I stumble from bed, cow-heavy and floral/ In my Victorian nightgown.').

Her last completed poem, 'Edge', imagines a dead woman arranged like an effigy on a tomb, beginning 'The woman is perfected'. The dead woman is described with her children, 'Each dead child coiled, a white serpent,/ One at each little/ Pitcher of milk'. Here Plath draws on Shakespeare's *Antony and Cleopatra*, where Cleopatra commits suicide by putting a poisonous snake to her breast, and then describes it as 'my baby at my breast/ That sucks the nurse asleep'. The implication of these images seems to be that motherhood in some sense kills women; that women's bodies are seen, not as valuable in themselves, but as functional for others (notably children), and that the world is not satisfied until women are destroyed completely; being 'dead' is being 'perfected'. Within a week of writing these lines, Plath had killed herself.

An understanding of the degree of social and cultural rebellion involved in Plath's most savage poems must be tempered by a recognition that her responses are extreme, rather than typical. Nor does her writing give much sense that she protests on behalf of women in general. Nevertheless, extreme cases may reveal typical cultural pressures; those whose powers of endurance are weakened succumb to them. Those who have claimed Plath's work for feminism have done so on the grounds that she exemplifies some of the 'wrongs of women', rather than that she herself has provided a feminist analysis of them.

The strength of Plath's work lies in its naked emotional force and in the originality of its imagery; that much of it is essentially private, and that it often has a dream-like or surrealistic quality merely aligns Plath with many other modern writers, including prose writers like Virginia Woolf.

This survey of women poets is inevitably very selective, and omits many fine poets, such as Christina Rossetti, who was not, by her own account, a feminist but provided intriguing symbolic accounts of women's sexuality in poems like 'Goblin Market' (1862). Others produced work which perhaps does not seem particularly 'womanly' like Marianne Moore (1887–1972), who wrote cool, thoughtful pieces, often about animals. There has also been considerably less critical work done on women poets than on women novelists. The best introduction is thus often an anthology with notes. The ideal anthology would include work by Asian, Caribbean and African women writing in English.

4 Fiction

As we have seen, it is in fiction that the contributions of women have been most conspicuous and most widely acknowledged. The novel evolved and established itself firmly in the course of the eighteenth century, and this development is generally thought to be related to the growth of the middle classes in the same period. Many newly-literate women had unprecedented amounts of leisure time at their disposal, in accordance with the notion that the wives and daughters of the newly-established 'gentlemen' were 'ladies' and therefore should not be engaged in productive or physical activity.[1]

As a novel-reading public grew, demands for new novels increased, and writing them became potentially profitable. A new institution, the circulating library, made novels available to subscribers for a relatively modest financial outlay, and a very high proportion of the patrons of such libraries were women. Therefore writers of novels very often chose subjects which might be thought appealing to women readers, and the love-and-marriage plot became a particularly common convention.

For some of the same reasons, the novel for some time was regarded with suspicion, or thought of as a genre inferior to poetry and drama. On the one hand cautious parents feared the effect on their daughters of reading 'romances' which in many cases had extravagant plots involving, not merely love and marriage, but defiance of convention, elopements, dangerous adventures, perhaps duels and deaths caused by passionate attachments. Some novels, including the Gothic, typically placed an unprotected heroine in danger of seduction, rape or forced marriage, and could easily be thought to awaken too much sexual curiosity and speculation in 'innocent' virgin readers. On the other hand, the very fact that novels were read by women no doubt contributed to what was, initially, their relatively low status.

The history of the development of the novel in the eighteenth and early nineteenth centuries is thus in some measure the history of its attempts to be taken seriously, and this struggle involved claims and justifications which in fact often were conflicting. In one direction, attempts were made to defend the use of romance as providing a level of experience above that of the merely mundane, the everyday. Conversely, assertions were made to the effect that the real province of fiction was not the world of extravagant romance, but that of realism, which was often said to be ill-served by drama and poetry. Finally, a moral function was sometimes claimed for the novel, not least for novels which might provide sheltered young women with 'awful warnings' about the dangers of the world outside the bourgeois home.

It is not necessary to take all of these various claims at face value with regard to every novel published. We still have with us today the argument that films, television programmes and videos which unquestionably have a sensational or shocking effect must nevertheless be allowed to circulate in the name of realism. The question of the influence of such material on the young and 'innocent' is as controversial today as it ever was. No doubt the motives – whether mainly artistic or mainly profit-orientated – of the creators and circulators of these works were as varied in the eighteenth century as they are today.

Among the many writers of popular novels in the eighteenth century there were a considerable number, indeed probably a majority, of women; but of these, only a few, including Fanny Burney and Maria Edgeworth, have generally been remembered, and little of their work has been widely available until quite recent years. Jane Spencer's *The Rise of the Woman Novelist* (1986) and Dale Spender's *Mothers of the Novel* (1986)[2] help to retrieve many of the 'lost' women writers and demonstrate that their contributions to the development of the genre, in terms of technique and subject matter, were often far more extensive and crucial than standard literary histories indicate. For example, Maria Edgeworth, who wrote novels about rural Ireland, is now recognized as the first 'regionalist' and as a crucial influence on later writers like Sir Walter Scott; love plots were decidedly secondary in her work.

Nevertheless, a great many of the women novelists did make extensive use of use of love-and-marriage plots. The fact that these plots, sometimes also involving a lone heroine abroad in a dangerous world, had also been used in England by male writers such as Daniel Defoe and Samuel Richardson, perhaps made it easier for women writers to choose this subject matter without necessarily being consigned automatically to a kind of women's literary ghetto. In the United States, by contrast, few men novelists of stature took up such subject matter, and it took correspondingly far longer before any American woman novelist was regarded as having achieved the standing of writers like Herman Melville and Mark Twain.

Women novelists had even more reasons than men for focusing on such issues in their plots. The economic situation of women in the eighteenth and nineteenth centuries automatically created a problem. Very few women were economically independent, as money and property tended to descend to men, a circumstance which is central in, for instance, Jane Austen's *Pride and Prejudice*. It is not strictly the case that no employment was available for women: working-class women, while scarcely secure economically, usually kept body and soul together by functioning as domestic servants, but middle- and upper-class women had very limited opportunities to achieve financial autonomy by their own efforts. Novel-writing in fact provided one of the few potential sources of income for respectable women, but could of course only be pursued by those with sufficient natural gifts. Most middle-class women were virtually forced to be dependent upon a male relative – father, brother, brother-in-law – or on a husband. In the upper classes there was usually enough money to go round, so that an unmarried woman was not an unbearable burden on the family's finances, but in the middle classes she could be a real financial problem. Even a woman who had achieved independent means by some form of inheritance had to watch out for men eager to take control of it by marrying her – for in most circumstances a woman's property became her husband's upon marriage. Thus marriage was an absolutely central determinant of a woman's position, and the question of whom she was to marry was crucial for her whole life.

For middle-class women, the norms of sexual morality insisted that sexual activity could take place only within marriage. In a sense this situation could be said to protect women, since pregnancy and motherhood outside marriage would be completely disastrous to a woman with no means of self-support. However, marriage itself was no complete guarantee of protection. Divorce was virtually unavailable to women until quite late in the nineteenth century, and therefore married women could be left at the mercy of brutal or indifferent husbands. Certainly the possibility of emotional or sexual satisfaction outside marriage was in effect non-existent for respectable middle-class women.

It is nevertheless striking how many eighteenth- and nineteenth-century novels by women have plots which imply a greater or lesser degree of optimism about the possibilities for an individual women to manoeuvre within these limits and achieve some degree of self-determination in spite of them. Many of these novelists are also very much preoccupied with the question of moral choice for women in very constrained circumstances. When women are so hemmed in on every side, it may often seem that they are the victims of circumstances and therefore no real options are available to them. On the other hand, if women cannot and therefore do not make significant choices and decisions, they do not act as fully human creatures and are by definition inferior to men.

Although, as we have seen, relatively few of the women novelists of the eighteenth century are remembered, in England the nineteenth century was a very rich period for women novelists, and many of them have virtually always enjoyed critical esteem. All of these major women novelists of the nineteenth century (including Jane Austen, the Brontë sisters, Elizabeth Gaskell and George Eliot) provide very clear depictions of the constraints within which their women protagonists act, but all at the same time insist that their women are capable of significant moral action – sometimes facing excruciating choices which have a distinctly moral character. In this sense their works could be described as feminist, in that they assert the full human value of their characters even though they may not make explicit pleas for legal and social reform.

The first to reach prominence, and enjoy an esteem which has endured from her own time to ours, was Jane Austen (1775–1817). Austen's plots, like those of many of the other women novelists of the eighteenth and nineteenth centuries, all have as a central character a marriageable young woman, of respectable origins but not from the upper class, and all involve some problem about her marriage; in Austen's case the problem is always solved happily.

In one sense Austen's work can be seen as putting an end to the previously-mentioned controversies about the value and place of the novel, the worthiness of its audience, the pretensions of its subject matter and its potential moral stature. Austen's work was widely acclaimed, not least famously by the Prince Regent, and therefore escaped the charge of being 'merely' or 'mainly' appropriate for the amusement of bored women. Austen herself tackled head-on the charge that the novel was an insignificant genre. In *Northanger Abbey* (1818), the narrator makes a now-famous defence, both of novels (including notably those written by women) and of their attention to women protagonists:

'Only a novel! . . . It is only Cecilia, or Camilla, or Belinda'; in short, only some work in which the greatest powers of the mind are displayed, in which the most thorough knowledge of human nature, the happiest delineations of its varieties, the liveliest effusions of wit and humour are conveyed to the world in the best chosen language.[3]

Austen's own work fits into the tradition of the realistic novel, deriving characters and settings from the kind of life she herself led as a member of a family of country gentry. In *Northanger Abbey* she pokes fun at the Gothic novel with its exotic settings and mysterious occurrences. She implicitly defended her own practice of limiting her settings to her own particular social group, a small group of characters and a restricted geographic range, when she described such material, 'three or four families in a country village' as 'the heart and beauty' of a book.[4] She compared her work to a 'little bit (two inches wide) of Ivory on which I work with so fine a brush.'[5] By implication, then, her art form was different from that with a larger scope, but had as great an aesthetic validity and required at least as much skill to execute.

Much of the popularity of Austen's work, from her own time until now, is doubtless based on the fact that it is mostly comic, but it is also unmistakably moral in its intentions, both because it upheld the conventional sexual morality of its time, and in the less obvious sense that it subjected everyday decisions and actions to scrutiny and criticism. Furthermore, by its concentration on the virtues of domestic life, it in effect defended the moral stature of the middle classes against the more dubious values of the aristocracy.

Although occasional readers have objected that Austen's scope is too narrow (not involving war and politics directly, for example), on the whole her work established that realistic treatments of the domestic life and romantic problems of the middle classes, notably middle-class women, provided ample material for artistic concentration. Her novels certainly cannot be called revolutionary; while they are frequently critical of individual characters, and sometimes may be read as criticizing certain social tendencies, on the whole her work accepts her society and shows her characters working within it. Indeed, one of the secrets of its popularity and general acceptability lies, no doubt, in the fact that it appeared to assert widely-held values such as the importance of family life, the obligation to behave respectfully toward one's parents (however unsatisfactory) and the necessity of chastity.

All of Austen's completed novels give evidence of the vital significance of marriage for women, especially middle-class women. The title character in *Emma* (1814) in fact observes that it is only a financially independent woman like herself who can freely choose to remain unmarried and contemplate the prospect with any satisfaction. Emma does of course marry, and Austen's less well-placed heroines in other novels are also 'rewarded' at the end of the story by marriages which in fact represent, not merely economic security, but a decided step up on the social and economic scale. Austen certainly has no time for the notion that marriages should be the result of romantic attachments, without reference to economic considerations.

Nevertheless marriage, however crucial economically for Austen's women, is far from being an unquestioned good. In *Pride and Prejudice*, most notably, a contrast is drawn between Mrs Bennet's eagerness to marry her daughters off to virtually any comer, and the far more critical attitude of Elizabeth; if her initial estimate of the aristocratic Mr Darcy as proud and unjust were a correct estimate, her refusal of him would likewise be appropriate, regardless of his avowed love for her and the social advantages involved in the marriage.

Similarly, the novel acknowledges that women without independent incomes have virtually no other resource than marriage, but appears to hold that this is not in itself a reason to marry if the prospective husband is otherwise unsuitable. The case of Charlotte Lucas presents plainly the dilemma of a woman unprovided for; no realistic alternative to marriage is offered within the novel (nor was there one available in the society of the time), yet Charlotte's decision to accept the appalling Mr Collins shocks the reader as much as it shocks Elizabeth, however 'reasonably' Charlotte defends herself and however clearly her dilemma is presented.

The three most important young woman in *Pride and Prejudice* (Elizabeth, her sister Jane, and Charlotte Lucas) are all shown as working within very limited circumstances. Yet the particular responses the young women make are seen as significant, and are subjected to value judgements. Elizabeth (who has two serious offers before she finally accepts one) refuses to marry for money and security only; respect and affection for her partner are seen as essential for a woman's own self-respect. Nor do considerations of family responsibility override this need for self-respect.

Charlotte, considerably older than Elizabeth, and apparently less attractive physically, is in much more stringent circumstances. While her acceptance of a dubious marriage is portrayed as understandable, it is hardly applauded. Yet Charlotte earns respect by sticking to the terms of her bargain, remaining loyal to her husband and allowing him a degree of dignity he has scarcely earned. Her intelligence and self-control are brought to bear, and the conclusion one is left with is that she has in a sense regained the moral stature lost by her decision to marry for money and security through being a *good* wife even though her husband is undeserving of her, and even though her decision to marry was not made in true freedom.

Jane suffers from an unreliable and thoughtless, if essentially well-meaning, lover. In Jane too, self-control is perceived as a primary virtue; her inability to blame anyone for anything is described by Elizabeth as 'angelic'. To give way to 'passion', including the sorrow of disappointed love, would be a failing, yet at the same time Jane's self-control is shown as contributing to her lover's confusion about her feelings and intentions. Jane 'earns' her marriage to Mr Bingley by her beauty and her virtues, including good nature and self-control. Yet for the reader, Jane's character is implicitly somewhat inferior to Elizabeth's, which involves greater intelligence, a highly-developed wit and critical sense and a willingness to take risks. Accordingly, the Elizabeth–Darcy marriage offers a promise for human fulfilment on more levels than the blander Jane–Bingley marriage.

Austen does not draw the simplistic conclusion (found attractive by, for example, Samuel Richardson) that women are 'naturally good' and men are likely to be morally suspect because of their sexual rapaciousness; rather, the actions, choices and relationships of both the men and the women characters are taken seriously and are subject to quite searching judgements. Furthermore, although Austen plainly deplores lack of chastity, as seen in Lydia, she accords her women characters a moral nature which is not confined to their sexual relationships. Miss Bingley's treatment of Elizabeth and Jane condemns her at least as much as does her relentless pursuit of Darcy. This insistence on the full moral existence of women is implicitly an insistence on the human equality of women with men.

Austen was well aware of the misery which could attend a gentlewoman living out her life without financial resources, as can be seen in *Persuasion* (1818) and *Emma*, but she does not explicitly condemn a social and economic order which permits it (indeed, attacks on the system of male primogeniture are voiced mainly by the mindless Mrs Bennet). Nevertheless, her assertion, through characters like Elizabeth, that women should hold out for marriages which provide emotional satisfaction and individual dignity, suggests that Austen believed that it was necessary for women to run the financial and social risks implicit in maintaining their self-respect. Only in *Emma*, one of her last novels, does Austen introduce, even tangentially, the possibility of a woman earning her living; by the early years of the nineteenth century the role of governess offered a very limited and generally unappealing, but nevertheless real, opportunity for women to achieve a degree of financial independence.

The experiences of governesses, or female teachers, accordingly provided significant material for Charlotte Brontë (1816–55) in her novels *Jane Eyre* and *Villette* (1853), and for her sister Anne in *Agnes Grey* (1847). Although the Brontë sisters had an extremely close family life, all of them experienced the difficulties of trying to make a living outside the home. Being a teacher provided an opportunity for a small measure of financial independence but domestic or institutional confinement generally went along with a teaching post and dependence upon one's own family was frequently replaced by being subject to the whims of one's employer.

Charlotte Brontë's novels in particular present the figure of a woman who must make her way without significant protection from family or friends, and in doing so she offers an even more radical presentation of the social and economic constraints upon middle class women than Jane Austen does. Austen's women risk, at worst, genteel poverty; Jane Eyre, at one point in the novel, is prepared to become a servant, literally becomes a beggar, and is at real risk of dying of hunger and exposure. Brontë, a minister's daughter, does not point out that the only real option for a woman in such a situation was prostitution, although her friend Elizabeth Gaskell, a minister's wife, was franker on this point in her novels *Mary Barton* and *Ruth*.

Nevertheless, the isolation of Charlotte Brontë's female protagonist effectively *forces* her into independence while her situation at best gives her a degree of freedom of choice not available to those who must answer to their families. Jane Eyre expresses directly her aspirations to an even wider life and greater fulfilment. Charlotte Brontë introduces explicit observations on the role and place of women:

It is vain to say human beings ought to be satisfied with tranquillity: they must have action and they will make it if they cannot find it. . . . Women are supposed to be very calm generally, but women feel just as men feel; they need exercise for their faculties and a field for their efforts as much as their brothers do; they suffer from too rigid a restraint, too absolute a stagnation, precisely as men would suffer. . . .[6]

The need for improved education for women was a major concern of many early feminists such as Mary Wollstonecraft whose *A Vindication of the Rights of Women* (1792) is a classic feminist text. For Charlotte Brontë, education is the key to such independence as Jane Eyre achieves (at least, until an inheritance comes along). Not only does it provide her with a means of earning a living, however modest; education also offers her an opportunity to explore her creative potential and gives her a sense of delight in accomplishment.

I toiled hard, and my success was proportionate to my efforts; . . . in less than two months I was allowed to commence French and drawing. . . . I feasted . . . on the spectacle of ideal drawings . . ., all the work of my own hands.[7]

Charlotte Brontë's work is thus, like Jane Austen's, firmly based in a real world of financial and economic constraints upon women, while it similarly endorses women's aspirations to something beyond domestic life. Jane Eyre and Elizabeth Bennet in *Pride and Prejudice*, although otherwise quite different characters, share one trait: a willingness to assert themselves in 'unfeminine' fashion against what they perceive as tyrannical, unreasonable or immoral impositions. Elizabeth stands up to Mr Collins and Lady Catherine de Bourgh, while Jane Eyre opposes a whole string of people determined to dominate her – mostly, but not only, men. Both characters furthermore pronounce upon their own sense of their equality with those who regard themselves as their superiors.

Such assertions in Austen's case have generally been seen as related to the growing moral and cultural self-confidence of the middle classes in her own time, but for Brontë such a sense of equality is ultimately based in religion. She appeals beyond the patriarchal and hierarchical order in this world to a higher order. In one of the most famous and frequently-cited passages in *Jane Eyre*, Jane stands up to Mr Rochester, her domineering employer and undeclared lover. The daringness of her confrontation of him lies only partly in her social and economic dependence upon him; she is also making a declaration of her love for him, a most 'unmaidenly' proceeding as he has not made his intentions plain. Even today there is a considerable taboo against a woman being the first to speak out in such circumstances.

'Do you think, because I am poor, obscure, plain and little, I am soulless and heartless? . . . I have as much soul as you, and full as much heart! . . . It is my spirit that addresses your spirit; just as if both had passed through the grave, and we stood at God's feet, equal, – as we are![8]

In both *Pride and Prejudice* and *Jane Eyre* the heroine is offered a respectable but loveless marriage which she rejects vehemently. Both authors would have agreed that love is necessary to a woman's integrity in marriage. But by contrast with Austen's restrained approach to the emotions associated with love, the most striking contribution Charlotte Brontë made to the development of the novel is her acknowledgement that women experience passion and her insistence that they are entitled to it – even if plain and humble.

Thus while retaining a foothold in the practical realities of women's situation, Charlotte Brontë adds to the novel many of the elements of a Romantic sensibility. Her plots include many situations more dangerous and extreme than any found in Jane Austen's work, her characters (especially male characters) are frequently far from prosaic, and hints of exotic experience often hover around them. The external world reflects the emotions of her main characters; elements in her plots sometimes recall Gothic novels like those of Ann Radcliffe (1764–1823). Charlotte Brontë thus provides a kind of marrying of the realistic and the romantic elements of the novel tradition which she inherited.

As is widely known, the Brontë sisters all published initially under supposedly neutral, but in fact masculine, pseudonyms; when it became known that the author of *Jane Eyre* was a woman, several influential readers, previously admirers of the work, felt that it was improper for a woman to have produced a novel so full of romantic emotion. Writing, as she was, in Victorian times, Charlotte Brontë was not altogether explicit about the physical components of love, yet there is no question but that her heroines are fully capable of – and desirous of – experiencing love in all its aspects.

Brontë's Jane Eyre also insists upon chastity according to traditional principles – partly, to be sure, in accord with her religious convictions. Yet in the novel chastity appears, not least, as an element in a woman's sense of her own value. The plot of *Jane Eyre* thus turns largely on the problem of reconciling sexuality and respectability. Mr Rochester, already married, offers the first, but only in adulterous terms; St John Rivers offers the second, but assures Jane, in one of literature's most resistable proposals of marriage, that she is 'formed for labour, not for love.' He gives the proposal a religious twist: 'I claim you – not for my pleasure, but for my Sovereign's service.'[9] Jane's rejection of him implies that although the dictates of conscience may require celibacy, a religious motive does not justify a passionless marriage.

The conflict is of course resolved in the ending of the novel, in which Jane, responding to a mystical summons, is reunited with the now-widowed Mr Rochester; it is less often noticed that by going to him in ignorance of his changed circumstances, Jane is in effect giving herself up to passion and running the risks involved in exposing herself to temptation again. In the event, the threatened conflict does not materialize.

The fiction of Charlotte and also Emily Brontë could be seen as providing a counterpart to the poetry of Keats and Byron, which gave primacy to sensuality and emotion. In acknowledging passion in women as well as men, the Brontës in effect insisted that realizing one's full potential included (but was not confined to) achieving the satisfaction of one's desires. It would, however, be misleading to indicate that major writers of the nineteenth – or any other – century confined themselves to love stories told from a woman's point of view. Many, including the Brontë sisters and George Eliot, and the early twentieth-century Americans Edith Wharton and Willa Cather, wrote works with masculine protagonists and narrators.

The Brontës and George Eliot were furthermore far from being the only women writers of the nineteenth century who chose to use masculine pseudonyms as a result of the well-founded belief that their work would be judged differently – and less liberally or favourably – if it were known to be by a woman, or that the use of a masculine or neutral pseudonym would facilitate the treatment of other subjects than love and marriage as seen from the point of view of a young woman. Among the many others who chose the same strategy were the Irish cousins Violet Martin and Edith Somerville, who published as 'E. OE. Somerville and Martin Ross', George Egerton (Mary Chavelita Dunne), and the early twentieth-century Australian novelist Henry Handel Richardson (Ethel Florence Lindesay Richardson) – none of whom, incidentally, specialized in love plots. The persistence of this practice of using non-feminine pseudonyms suggests that, despite the considerable and widely-recognized achievements of women in writing fiction in the nineteenth century, the position of women writers in relation to critics and to the reading public was always rather precarious.

Likewise, the recognition accorded to the 'major' women novelists of the nineteenth century should not be allowed to distract from the fact that, in the nineteenth as in the eighteenth century, a great many other women wrote works which have been allowed to fall into an undeserved obscurity.

It has earlier been mentioned that English women novelists were among the first to bring 'the industrial theme' and a treatment of the lives of the working classes into fiction. In America, during the last quarter of the nineteenth century, women like Kate Chopin, Mary Wilkins Freeman and Sarah Orne Jewett created a literature based on their knowledge of the distinctive cultures of particular regions of the United States. Labelled 'Regionalist', the work of these women has until fairly recently been assumed to be minor, perhaps not least because they specialized in short stories and often wrote about women, although William Faulkner, for example, has not been thought less significant for writing almost exclusively about Mississippi. Certainly these women writers helped to establish that the regional variety of the United States provides for the possibility of a literature which is very rich and varied, not least linguistically. Kate Chopin's *The Awakening* is now regarded as a masterpiece of its period.

In Britain, women made other contributions to the development of fiction. It is generally agreed that the great strength of the nineteenth-century novel, both in Britain and elsewhere in Europe, lies in its realistic depiction of approximately contemporary life although individual novels also include Gothic, romantic, historical and symbolic elements; the novels and novelists we have thus far considered in detail fit into this larger tradition. Later, around the turn of the twentieth century, women made vital, and in some cases, long-ignored contributions to the development of the modernist novel. A recent study shows that largely-forgotten women novelists of the 1880s and 1890s engaged in experiments in the form of the novel; while these were only partially successful, they probably helped to prepare for more satisfactory efforts by later writers.[10]

Essential to modernism is attention to an inner, rather than an external, reality, and it is implicit that modernism requires forms and techniques different from those employed in realistic fiction. Credit for establishing modernism in English fiction has traditionally been accorded to James Joyce and Virginia Woolf, but more recently increasing recognition has been given to the pioneering efforts of Dorothy Richardson (1873–1957). Richardson wrote a sequence of thirteen novels, several of them quite short, which are collectively known under the title *Pilgrimage*. All are concerned with the efforts of Miriam Henderson, an alter ego for Richardson herself, to achieve an identity and an independent status after financial reversals in her family force her out of the conventional role of a 'gentleman's daughter'. The first twelve novels were written and published over a period of more than twenty years, beginning in 1915, while the last was not published until 1967, ten years after Richardson's death.

Although the component works were published separately, Richardson herself apparently regarded them as 'chapters' in a long novel rather than as independent items. Each work does form a unit in the sense that there is a reason why it starts and stops where it does, but taken together they follow Miriam Henderson's life in chronological order. The works offer, at best, little exposition, so that it is difficult to start reading in the middle of the sequence.

Writing fiction in this way obviously involves a departure from conventional notions of plot and structure; *Pilgrimage* has a distinct forward movement but provides relatively little sense of complications which are created and then resolved in order to bring about a rounding-off and ending of the story. Such departures from traditional notions of plot and narrative are now seen as being characteristic of modernist works; something else is substituted for the interest provided, in earlier novels, by the 'story'.

What Richardson attends to instead is the impressions Miriam receives of the world and people around her, and her reflections upon these. Apparently trivial and transient experiences are often treated in as great detail as those which might be thought crucial for Miriam's progress. The work which gradually evolves is a landmark in the development of the 'stream-of-consciousness' technique in English.

A matter which becomes increasingly important in Miriam's considerations is that of the difference between men's and women's standards and values. Perhaps surprisingly, Richardson was not a political feminist, although she wrote her first works in the period in which women were engaged in crucial struggles for the right to vote and to take university degrees. She was rather what we might call a cultural feminist, affirming the value of women's experience and women's responses to life. As *Pilgrimage* developed, she produced increasingly sharp reactions to the notion that men's standards and men's view of women are assumed to be normative.

It ought to be illegal to publish a book by a man without first giving it to a woman to annotate. But what was the answer to men who called women inferior because they had not invented or achieved in science or art? On whose authority had men decided that science and art were greater than anything else? The world could not go on until this question had been answered. Until then, until it had been clearly explained that men were always and always partly wrong in their ideas, life would be full of poison and secret bitterness. Men fight about their philosophies and religions, there is no certainty in them; but their contempt for women is flawless and unanimous.[11]

The account of Miriam's life and slow development in *Pilgrimage* includes some love interest and involves the question of whom Miriam is to marry – if anyone. But this issue is not particularly central; Miriam is rather concerned with establishing for herself ways in which she can lead a fulfilling life *outside of* the conventional institutions of domesticity, and the other single women whom she encounters do not always provide encouraging models.

Virginia Woolf recognized the revolutionary nature of what Dorothy Richardson was doing, although her praise for the result was not unequivocal. She realized that Richardson was doing away with conventional elements of fiction: 'The reader is not provided with a story; he [*sic*] is invited to embed himself in Miriam Henderson's consciousness.' Where Woolf was dubious was in the quality of the insights Richardson achieved with her new techniques. 'Sensations, impressions, ideas and emotions glance off her, unrelated and unquestioned, without shedding as much light as we had hoped into the hidden depths.'[12] As in her praise of Jane Austen for creating a 'woman's sentence,' which we have previously discussed, Woolf laid particular importance on Richardson's distinctive style.

She has invented . . . a sentence which we might call the psychological sentence of the feminine gender. . . . It is a woman's sentence, but only in the sense that it is used to describe a woman's mind by a writer who is neither proud nor afraid of anything that she may discover in the psychology of her sex.[13]

While Woolf's description of Richardson's 'sentence' may seem no more enlightening than her description of Jane Austen's, she does indirectly call our attention to the fact that Richardson felt free to write sentences which were fragmentary, allusive, or sometimes very long and apparently disconnected, in recognition that our mental processes do not occur in the language of public discourse.

An obvious conclusion to draw is that, even if it is correct that Richardson's work ultimately lacks a 'profundity' to which Woolf aspired, her example certainly seems to have challenged Woolf to see if she herself could make use of similar techniques to better effect. The present judgement of most critics is no doubt that Woolf's accomplishment is the 'greater', but the revival of interest in Richardson's work serves as a reminder that most writers work in a more or less conscious recognition of the existence and achievement of their predecessors and contemporaries. There is little direct evidence that James Joyce, for example, read Richardson's work; nevertheless she certainly contributed to the climate of experimentation and change in which he laboured.

Virginia Woolf (1882–1941) herself was a literary critic and essayist as well as a writer of fiction. In two famous and influential essays, 'Modern Fiction' (1919) and 'Mr Bennett and Mrs Brown' (1924) she expressed her own ideas about what was appropriate for fiction. She disliked the work of contemporaries such as John Galsworthy, H. G. Wells, and Arnold Bennett on the grounds that they were mainly interested in what she tends to call 'facts', that is, what can be observed externally. She calls these writers 'materialists' who are 'not concerned with the spirit but with the body.'[14] In her terms, their understanding of the psychology of their characters was thus oversimplified and therefore false.

In her own work, Woolf is also little interested in external events for their own sake; in this she is rather unlike Dorothy Richardson, for although Richardson presents in great detail Miriam Henderson's mental and emotional reactions to external events and characters, her responses are nevertheless largely concerned with understanding and evaluating these. For Woolf, what is 'outside' is frequently little more than a trigger for a character's reveries, which take on a life of their own, moving freely through time and space until the surrounding 'present moment' is virtually forgotten.

Woolf is however more like Richardson in that the element of conventional plot in most of her works is minimal; these two writers carry much further a tendency which can also be seen in such male contemporaries as D. H. Lawrence. Woolf's shorter works often give particularly clear examples of distinctive tendencies in her writing. Often there is considerable question as to whether these can be called 'stories'. Sometimes they lack a sense of character as much as of plot. Perhaps they are better described as essays or 'sketches', rather than stories.

Fairly typical of these short works is 'The Mark on the Wall' (1917); a woman notices a mark on the wall of her sitting room and wonders what it is. The narration is a record of a thought process, a kind of meditation, which is set going by this particular external stimulus, but then proceeds according to the concerns, the past experiences and the character of the woman who is sitting and thinking. Her meditation very soon moves far away from the question of what the mark on the wall 'really' (that is, factually) is.

The text is *in itself* concerned with the question of how important the world of 'fact' is; the question of *what* the mark is, is much less important than the thought process it provokes. In the course of the narrative, the narrator's meditation is repeatedly drawn back to this factual question, but she seems reluctant to get up and look at the mark more closely so as to arrive at an answer. When the 'truth' about the mark becomes known at the end (it is a snail), the story also stops. Something is finished, even destroyed, by this factual information.

On the other hand the loss of contact with the 'real' world also seems to be dangerous. At certain points the narrator wants her thoughts to go in some other direction than the one they have taken by themselves. This problem is seen partly in terms of childhood and early training – one is *trained* to think of the world as decided, definite, orderly and fixed. Everything has a place and an arbitrary set of relationships, represented in the narrator's meditation by 'Whitaker's Table of Precedence', which determines the relative importance of the Archbishop of Canterbury, the Lord High Chancellor, and the Archbishop of York.

Elements of Woolf's feminism emerge here; she tended to associate the world of 'fact', science, and arbitrary order with men, that of intuition, insight, art and the creation of emotional harmony with women. A life based on a search for 'facts' is satirized in the description of a retired colonel who spends his energy trying to determine whether certain mounds on the South Downs are tombs or camps. He 'decides', but he never really finds out. Woolf seems to be suggesting that the real problem is not so much the search for facts as the belief that one can always arrive at them. Often what are presented as 'facts' are merely opinions or prejudices elaborately defended, no more valuable than the 'unscientific' wanderings of the mind; there is a point relevant to feminism here as well.

On the other hand, although the prevailing 'system' is shown by implication to be nonsensical, the narrator in 'The Mark on the Wall' becomes anxious at prolonged loss of contact with it. Certainly there is some ambivalence here, and it is hard, in this context, to forget that Woolf suffered episodes of what then was called 'madness'; she finally committed suicide during one such episode. An exact modern clinical diagnosis of her illness is disputed, and in any case needs to be seen in the light of recent feminist discussion of the tendency to label women as 'mentally ill' when they are unable to adjust to the demands of a patriarchal society.[15] Nevertheless, it is not surprising that Woolf's work should express some fear at complete immersion into the self, complete loss of contact with the external world.

Perhaps what 'The Mark on the Wall' ultimately suggests is that what is needed is some kind of balance between awareness of the external world and attention to the internal world; the snail, with its hard outside shell and its soft interior, may be a symbol of the combination of the two. Elsewhere, explicitly in *A Room of One's Own* and implicitly in her novel *Orlando* (1928), (in which the main character lives for almost four centuries and undergoes a change of sex) Woolf expressed a need for a merging of the characteristics thought of as 'masculine' with those thought of as 'feminine'. The resulting nature could be described as 'androgynous' (from Greek *andro*, male, and *gyn*, female).

Virginia Woolf was explicitly political and feminist in a way that Dorothy Richardson was not; in *Three Guineas* (1938), in a climate of approaching war, she laid the blame for wars and injustice on male domination, on the effects of allowing 'masculine' values to prevail. The ideal of androgyny was thus, for her, one which could save the human race from ultimate destruction; certainly, in her view, promoting this ideal was ultimately as much in the interests of men as of women. Some believe that her suicide was an expression of despair after the war finally broke out.

The concept of androgyny has become a controversial one. Some feminist scholars have been interested to explore it further, both in Woolf's own work and elsewhere in literature (not necessarily by women), [16] and some feminists see this ideal of uniting 'masculine' and 'feminine' characteristics in each individual as a solution for the problems caused by male domination and female subjugation. Others view the idea as a distraction from feminist aims, considering that it implies that there is something 'wrong' or 'incomplete' about women as they are; these feminists prefer to regard the problem as lying, not in the characteristics women (or men) have today, but in the fact that women are not treated justly in societies dominated legally and economically by men.

Virginia Woolf's work has always been highly respected, by men as well as by women, as making a unique contribution to the development of the possibilities of fictional form and subject matter. The extent to which her work is suffused by her feminist outlook was nevertheless long underplayed or ignored, but has in recent years been highlighted by feminist critics, whether they share her ideal of androgyny or not.

As we have already seen, there have always been women novelists, from the earliest days of novel writing, and there have always been women readers for novels; there have furthermore always been women novelists who wrote largely or almost exclusively for a female readership. In our own time it may easily seem to be the case that we are in a particularly 'golden' period for women novelists, although scholars repeatedly assure us that in fact we have just lost sight of many of the fine novelists of earlier generations.

It is however unquestionably true that at present women writers have become more conspicuous and are receiving greater serious attention and publicity than they did, for example, thirty years ago. It is no longer automatic to assume that women who write, very possibly about and for women, can largely be dismissed as less than truly serious. Not least, publishers have realized that there is a very substantial market for what is sometimes called 'serious women's fiction'.

In the ensuing richness, it is difficult to single out a particular living writer as 'representative' of her time. Nevertheless, one whose career has been followed with growing interest and increasing respect for the past twenty years, is Margaret Drabble (1939–). Drabble has been referred to as a 'chronicler-novelist'; that is, the cumulative impression which is created by Drabble's work is that it provides, in literary terms, a kind of social history of the educated middle classes in England in the period from about 1960 until the present.

Drabble, who was a brilliant undergraduate, could have had a career as a literary scholar; she is the editor of the 1985 edition of *The Oxford Companion to English Literature*, which is notable, not least, for having given much greater space to entries about literature by women than was found in the earlier editions of this standard reference work. She has always freely acknowledged her interest in literature by other women and has praised both predecessors and contemporaries; that is to say, she writes in consciousness of being part of a women's tradition in English literature.

Drabble has, directly and indirectly, expressed her own particular admiration for George Eliot, who, in her monumental *Middlemarch* (1871–72) attempted what is often described as a 'broad canvas', depicting English provincial life in the private sphere while at the same time showing the effects of political and economic change on individuals and the society as a whole. Eliot wrote sometimes from a woman's, sometimes from a man's point of view, and often her middle-aged characters are amongst the most vivid, even in works like *The Mill on the Floss* (1860) in which the protagonist is young. In all of these respects Margaret Drabble writes in the tradition of George Eliot.

Drabble's work cannot be described as autobiographical, but she has, especially in her earlier novels, used protagonists whose life situations in one or more respects closely resembled her own: a recent Oxford graduate in her first novel, *A Summer Bird-Cage* (1963), the wife of an actor and mother of young children in *That Garrick Year* (1964), a promising scholar from an earnestly liberal background in *The Millstone* (1965), an ambitious young woman from the North of England who has moved to London in *Jerusalem the Golden* (1967). Several of her later works are however not confined to a single protagonist, but offer a narrative with a multiple perspective and a corresponding increase in range and variety. *The Needle's Eye* (1972) is the first of Drabble's novels to be told partly from the point of view of a man; *The Realms of Gold* (1975) does have one main character but also follows several others, including both men and women, one of whom is lower middle class; *The Ice Age* (1977) divides its narrative almost equally among five different characters of both sexes, with several others also given more passing attention.

Generally, however, Drabble's characters have tended to become older as she herself has done, and to have experienced vicissitudes of life, such as divorce, the deaths of parents, changes of career, even imprisonment, which generally come after one's first youth. Thus in *The Middle Way* (1980), for example, the protagonist has a demanding career and a love life as well, but is also much concerned with her relationship with her virtually grown-up children; she furthermore lives in the multi-racial, multi-ethnic world of Britain in the 1980s, in contrast to earlier protagonists such as Emma in *That Garrick Year*, who appears to inhabit an exclusively Anglo-Saxon society.

Thus while Drabble's work started out looking as if it might fall into the tradition of novels essentially about young women, with an emphasis on their problems of love, marriage and, perhaps, careers, she has developed into a writer whose subject has become modern Britain, both public and private – with full, but far from exclusive, emphasis on the experiences of women in that context. Certainly she retains a perspective which is largely that of the educated middle classes; nor does she, for example, attempt to write in detail about West Indians in South London, yet her viewpoint has changed, and opened, as British society has changed.

Drabble is scarcely alone in having extended the range of the novel beyond the love-and-marriage plot; as we have seen, nineteenth-century women novelists did so too, and one remembers that more recently Virginia Woolf focused on middle-aged women in works like *Mrs Dalloway* and *To The Lighthouse*. Yet even more directly than these earlier writers, Drabble acknowledges that women continue to have love lives (and sex lives) despite the fact that they are beyond the Cinderella stage. The recognition of the women's market – and of the fact that money is often in the hands of middle-aged women – may have contributed to the growing use of such subject matter, in other writers such as Penelope Mortimer and Fay Weldon.

An element of Drabble's work which has been noticed by almost all her critics is that she is concerned with morality, although, like her most illustrious predecessors, including

George Eliot, she understands this to mean something far more complex than upholding conventional standards. *The Needle's Eye* has two protagonists, a gentle, conscientious lawyer, Simon Camish, who is unhappily married, and a divorced heiress, Rose Bryanston Vassiliou, who, when the novel opens, has given away almost all her money and lives in shabby contentment with her children. Through Rose, in particular, Drabble explores the question of the responsibility of the well-off for the less fortunate, of the descendants of imperial power for their erstwhile colonial subjects.

Rose has defied her parents by eloping with a passionate, flamboyant Greek of whom they disapprove; to everyone's surprise he proves to be successful financially, but Rose in time cannot bear the destructiveness of their quarrels, and leaves him. Her youthful rebellion against her parents thus fails to vindicate a romantic, as opposed to prudential, approach to life.

Rose furthermore feels her inherited wealth is a moral burden; she is quite easily persuaded to donate it to the cause of building a school in an African country, but the man who persuaded her turns some of the money to his own uses and the school is very soon destroyed in a civil war. This situation dramatizes what is often felt as a dilemma. Surely one should attempt to deploy one's resources wisely, rather than throw money away; giving freely involves risks, and may be merely foolish. On the other hand, the recipient must be accorded the right (and dignity) of full determination over the gift; anything else is demeaning, betraying essentially patriarchal attitudes.

Rose does not regret her gift, but for somewhat different reasons: without wealth, she feels free – of responsibility, and of guilt. She is much attracted to the apparently unromantic, phlegmatic, self-effacing Simon, who stays in a stultifying marriage out of a sense of responsibility to his perennially dissatisfied wife. The ending of the novel is a surprise: Simon and Rose, apparently 'meant for each other', do not come together. Instead, Rose returns to her husband, neither out of love for him, nor out of a sense that it is 'for the sake of the children', but rather out of the feeling that she has no right to deprive her husband of these children, who are as much his as hers. In doing so, however, she destroys her own peace of mind and soul, and becomes ill-tempered and abrasive.

From a feminist perspective, Rose's decision may seem

unpalatable in that it apparently gives her husband's rights and needs absolute priority over her own. This conclusion is however tempered by being put into the context of Simon's similar decision; it is also implicitly related to the larger, political context with its questions about the responsibilities of those who have the greatest advantages. Perhaps advantages are not always obvious. Perhaps Rose's *capacity* for peace and happiness, in itself, is a privilege.

Drabble can however scarcely be called anti-feminist, and she herself later expressed some doubts about the ending of *The Needle's Eye*.[17] In later novels, including notably *The Realms of Gold*, she presents divorced and independent women who have plainly made a correct decision. And if Rose is something of a perverse secular saint, she is matched by Anthony Keating in *The Ice Age*, a property speculator (the quintessential modern scoundrel, one would have thought) who winds up in an East European labour camp where he apparently achieves a kind of spiritual exaltation.

Rather, Drabble is refreshing in being a moralist who is conscious of existing standards but never merely accepts them. She prefers an exploration of the ironies, of the points at which neither conventional morality nor contemporary 'enlightenment' provide responses adequate to complexity of the questions. By always including, but not confining herself to, female protagonists, she silently reasserts the premise of earlier novelists like Austen, Charlotte Brontë and George Eliot. It is not merely that women, too, have a moral nature; rather, the experience of women, not least their moral experience, is essential to a full understanding of what it is to be human and to choose.

5 Drama

As we have seen earlier, it has been even more difficult for women to achieve acceptance as dramatists than in other genres. It is therefore intriguing to note that the one dramatist for whom we have any text at all between the end of the Roman theatre in the first century and the popular religious drama of the High Middle Ages is a tenth-century Saxon nun whom we know by the name Hroswitha, who wrote lively comedies in Latin, modelled on the plays of Terence. These were evidently performed by the nuns of her convent, and are another reminder that convent life gave women certain opportunities which they would not have enjoyed in the larger community.

In terms of English-language drama, women were first allowed to participate in theatrical life at the end of the seventeenth century, as a result of the restoration of Charles II to the throne in 1660. Charles had spent his exile in France, where there was a lively theatre life which included actresses, and he and his courtiers brought this institution back to England with them. The most characteristic plays of the period were comedies with complicated plots generally dependent upon sexual intrigue; the dialogue was characteristically racy, and *double entendres* were a major part of the fun. Not surprisingly, women who participated in the theatre were regarded as being rather less than respectable.

As we have already seen, Aphra Behn was one significant woman who contributed to this dramatic revival, and her plays are quite on a par with those of most of the male dramatists of the period. Aphra Behn wrote comedies as full of courtesans, fornication, and suggestive metaphors as those of men like William Wycherley. *The Rover* (1677) is set in Naples in carnival time, perhaps largely because of the possibilities provided by disguises and masks, and because the setting allows for the open appearance of courtesans and prostitutes. Its plot turns to some extent on problems which might be found anywhere in Europe in the period: those of young women who don't want to do what their male relatives have planned for them. One is being urged to marry an unattractive suitor for money, another is intended for a convent although all her instincts are, to put it mildly, secular. Of course they get their own way, although one can scarcely take seriously the idea that the aristocratic Hellena will be happy married to her pirate. Nor, to be sure, is one meant to; the point is that youthful rebels always win in comedies.

The most memorable character in the play is however the courtesan Angellica, making her living by means of her one asset, her beauty, yet giving herself freely to the attractive 'rover'. Her bitterness at his inconstancy shadows what is otherwise a lighthearted romp and perhaps sets off some vibrations in the spectator's mind about the connections between sex, love, money, property and marriage. The modern reader is also struck by the fact that attitudes toward 'gentlewomen' are blatantly different from attitudes to 'common' women. The unpropertied Aphra Behn certainly would have understood the problems of the 'working girl'.

The Rover was one of Behn's most popular pieces, and continued to be played until the later eighteenth century found it too improper, but the success of this and her other work did not prevent Aphra Behn's dying impoverished. She is nevertheless buried in Westminster Abbey, and Virginia Woolf observed 'All women together ought to let flowers fall upon the tomb of Aphra Behn . . . for it was she who earned them the right to speak their minds.'[1]

Between Aphra Behn and the twentieth century there were some other women dramatists, often apparently women who were also actresses, but most of these remain obscure to us. Some women writers of fiction also had their works dramatized; probably the most popular single play of the second half of the nineteenth century was a dramatization of Ellen (Mrs Henry) Wood's *East Lynne* (1861), a moralizing family drama.

The Irish Literary Revival turned up one remarkable woman dramatist, Augusta, Lady Gregory (1852–1932). Lady Gregory was an Anglo-Irishwoman, widowed young, who felt a particular responsibility for the tenants on her husband's estate and learned the Irish language so as to be able to communicate with them. She began to record the legends and stories she heard from them, and tried to write these in English in a way which would give something of the flavour of the Irish idiom.

Like so many other women of aristocratic origin, Lady Gregory did not initially write for publication, but she moved in nationalist circles where poets like W. B. Yeats were producing a consciously Irish literature, and she joined enthusiastically in their plans for establishing a national theatre for Ireland.

The new theatre needed plays, and Augusta Gregory, who was practical and a 'doer', therefore set out to help to provide them. In time she produced more than forty plays, some of which remain among the most popular in the Irish repertoire. Although she wrote on a variety of topics, and took tragic material from ancient Irish legends, her most popular works were one-act comedies, sometimes with a strong nationalist slant, such as *Spreading the News*, *The Rising of the Moon* and *The Workhouse Ward*. In addition to her fine sense of comic character, her distinctive contribution to Irish drama was in lively and vivid dialogue reflecting the actual speech of the Irish countryside, based on the language she had evolved to convey the dialect of her local district, Kiltartan.

Lady Gregory continued to manage Ireland's national theatre, the Abbey, almost until the time of her death. She also encouraged and collaborated with other major dramatists, including Yeats, J. M. Synge, and Sean O'Casey (who acknowledged that he might never have had a career without her.) For a time she was rather eclipsed by these other figures, although recent scholarship has demonstrated that she contributed far more than was originally supposed to some of the work of Yeats. Recent republications of her work have enhanced her reputation; her popularity with ordinary Irish theatregoers has never declined.

In general the American theatre has been somewhat more hospitable to women dramatists than the English, and in the twentieth century there are at least a few women's names which turn up fairly frequently in collections of representative plays, although several of these are remembered mainly for one play. Susan Glaspell's *Trifles* (1916) shows how two women can explain a death which has baffled the police, because of their understanding of household routines. Carson McCullers (who is also known for her fiction) gives a sympathetic portrayal of puberty in *A Member of the Wedding* (her own 1950 dramatization of an earlier novel). A striking number of black women have produced memorable literature, not least drama, in our century; the most famous is Lorraine Hansberry, whose *Raisin in the Sun* (1959), about the conflicting aspirations of a black family in Chicago, was a considerable commercial success. More recent black dramatists include Ntozake Shange and Alice Childress.

The major American woman dramatist of the first half of the century was however Lillian Hellman (1907–84). Her plays include many powerful and memorable women characters, but have sometimes been felt to be hostile to women, as few of them are portrayed as heroic, sympathetic or saintlike. But some feminists offer alternative interpretations of a character like Regina in *The Little Foxes* (1939), who outdoes the men of her family in scheming to take control: a woman like Regina is embittered because her considerable energies are given no outlet in Southern society, which expects women to be decorative, not active or productive.

Hellman's *The Children's Hour* (1934) presents her most obviously appealing female characters, as well as a rather incredible malevolent little girl. It was the first American play to give serious treatment to the subject of lesbianism, and is perhaps remembered chiefly for that innovation. It also presents an almost exclusively female world which includes energetic, accomplished women, and it explores an attractive female friendship with is destroyed by the accusation (and eventual admission) of lesbianism. Hellman seems neutral on the matter of lesbianism itself; her point is rather that single women are regarded with suspicion in a patriarchal culture. Even forceful and competent women defer to the one man in the play, whom they expect to resolve their difficulties; in this they are disappointed.

In general Hellman opposed narrow-mindedness and conventionality; she took a brave stand during the McCarthy attacks on American artists and intellectuals in the 1950s. It is therefore not surprising that her women are very likely to be the victims of such pressure to conform.

Women's involvement in the theatre has expanded greatly during the last twenty years in the English-speaking countries. Some of this activity is explicitly feminist, involving all-women theatre groups, for example, while other women dramatists have written for a more general public. Almost all of the recent women dramatists write in consciousness of the feminist revival of the 1970s and 1980s, although they do not all write exclusively about women. A radical political consciousness is notable, however, in the works of many of these women on both sides of the Atlantic. The first protest plays about the Vietnam war were, for example, written by women: Megan Terry's *Viet Rock* (1966) and Barbara Garson's *MacBird* (1966).

One of the most successful of these is Pam Gems (1925–   ), whose *Dusa, Fish, Stas and Vi* (1976) was first produced outside the commercial theatres of London's West End but, because of its critical and public success, later transferred to a commercial theatre. Gems herself says that another of her plays, *Queen Christina* (1977), had previously been rejected by a major London theatre on the grounds that it would 'appeal chiefly to women'. As she observes, no one is known to have rejected a play on the grounds that it would appeal chiefly to men.[2]

The apparently curious title of *Dusa, Fish, Stas and Vi* is made up simply of the names of the four characters who appear in it; they are four women who share a flat. Gems says that she was attempting to portray the situation of women at a particular historical moment; it is notable that all of the characters are still relatively young, and one has children, but none of them fits into the stereotype of what is 'typical' for women in their age range: the married mother of young children. Equally, none fits into another possible stereotype, that of the dedicated or ambitious career woman who has no sexual life. The play reflects actual demographic changes in modern Britain, where only a small percentage of people now live in the classic 'nuclear family' of mother, father and minor children; a variety of alternative living arrangements, like the one shown in the play, have become widespread for economic and other reasons.

Stas, who is professionally ambitious, in fact finances her education as a marine biologist by working as a well-paid call girl. Each of the other three women experiences a major emotional crisis in the play: Dusa's ex-husband kidnaps her children; Vi is anorexic, drug-taking and potentially suicidal;

the radical activist Fish's lover abandons her for a more conventional woman. Unable to accept this loss, she finally kills
herself.

The four women are given more or less equal treatment in
the play; this in itself reflects some of the values which came to
the fore in the earlier stages of the women's movement in the
1970s, when many women's groups resisted the hierarchical
organization (with elected officers and leaders of various
ranks) common to men's bodies; the women instead preferred
a 'flat' organization and communal responsibility, and had the
custom of using only Christian names, as in Gems's play.

The play poses in another form the contemporary question
of whether women can 'have it all' – artistic or intellectual
activity, a career, domestic life, children, romantic love, sexual
fulfilment. Certainly within the play none of the women
achieves all these things, or indeed more than one or two of
them. Nor does the play present any solutions. Fish's suicide is
the ultimate gesture of despair at the impossibility of becoming
an integrated person; her radicalism offers her no solution to
her emotional dependence upon an obviously unsatisfactory
man. The play concludes with her moving farewell letter to the
other women, which ends 'My loves, what are we to do? We
won't do as they want any more, and they hate it. What are we
to do?'[3]

Despite this note of despair, and its question of whether
women and men can continue to relate to each other, the play
does show positive elements in the lives of the characters. In
particular these four disparate women, who do not necessarily
even like each other very much, take turns at being the com-
forters and supporters as crises arise for the various characters.
The dialogue has an attractive witty, sardonic quality at the
same time that it is capable of strong emotional expression; it
perhaps suggests a quality of mind which has evolved to meet
the situation of new frustrations, new challenges.

As Gems says, her play is of a particular historical movement. To some extent we have moved beyond it; the idea that
women are not mainly or merely wives and mothers is one
which is now much more generally acknowledged than was
the case in 1976. Women participate more extensively in the
British theatre today, not least as directors and dramatists. And
theatrical managements are perhaps now somewhat more
aware that women make up the largest portion of most theatre

audiences; in any event several of Gems's later plays have had considerable commercial success, along with those of other dramatists such as Caryll Churchill and Nell Dunn.

Reading plays is really only an adjunct to seeing them; people who have an opportunity to do so will find they offer much more than can be suggested on the printed page.

6 Other Genres

We have seen some of the obstacles which prevented women from writing or publishing in the conventional genres, but we are becoming increasingly aware of how much of women's creative, literary activity has gone into forms which have usually been thought of as sub-literary, or extra-literary. Even though writing poetry or drama for publication or performance was frowned upon, letters were an entirely acceptable form of writing for ladies, and diaries or journals also offered an outlet. That these forms have a literary potential is confirmed by the fact that a great many of the earliest novels take the form of either letters, such as Samuel Richardson's *Pamela* (1741) or journals, such as Daniel Defoe's *Robinson Crusoe* (1719) and *A Journal of the Plague Year* (1722), which many believed were authentic documents rather than works of fiction.

One of the best known of the early letter writers is Dorothy Osborne (1627–95). She herself believed that it was embarrassing for a lady to publish, and criticized her contemporary, the Duchess of Newcastle, for bringing out poems. Of Osborne herself, Virginia Woolf said 'Had she been born in 1827, Dorothy Osborne would have written novels; had she been born in 1527, she would never have written at all.' Woolf adds, 'The art of letter-writing is often the art of essay-writing in disguise.'

We owe Dorothy Osborne's letters to a circumstance which was unhappy for her, if felicitous for the reader. She and Sir William Temple fell in love, but neither of them had a fortune, and both their families assumed that they would marry for money, Dorothy's brother in particular putting her under constant pressure to agree to one or other suitor whom he recommended.

As a result she and Temple were apart for about six years, seeing each other only occasionally; Dorothy's letters to Temple for the last two years have survived. We lack his side of the correspondence, but hers alone makes an appealing love story, with many incidental complications, vividly realized supporting characters, and illuminating glimpses of everyday life. It is, indeed, the kind of material that novels were made of 150 years later. The financial difficulties were eventually resolved and the couple were finally married in 1654 – ironically, just after Dorothy recovered from a disfiguring attack of smallpox.

The story is of course romantically attractive in itself; but so is Dorothy's personality as it emerges from the letters. The conventions of the time did not allow for strong expressions of passion from ladies, but she nevertheless conveys the force of her emotions with a restrained but lyric precision:

When I have supped I go into the garden and so to the side of a small river that runs by it where I sit down and wish you with me . . . in earnest 'tis a pleasant place and would be much more to me if I had your company. I sit there sometimes till I am lost with thinking and were it not for some cruel thoughts of the crossness of our fortunes that will not let me sleep there, I should forget there were such a thing to be done as going to bed.[2]

However, she also possessed a sharp wit, frequently brought to bear in her descriptions of other people, such as one much older, persistent suitor, Sir Justinian Isham, who quickly becomes 'The Emperor'. At the same time her devotion to Temple had a quality of nobility about it. She tried to bring herself to face the possibility of disappointment without bitterness. Considering that Temple might be forced to marry someone else, she writes (reporting a conversation with her brother):

I . . . said if I knew any woman that had a great fortune and were a person worthy of you, I should wish her you with all my heart. But Sister, says he, would you have him love her? Do you doubt it, would I say – he were not happy in it else.[3]

After their marriage we have few letters, but evidence suggests that they were as happy together as they had hoped to be.

Later, Dorothy's husband engaged as secretary the young Jonathan Swift, who respected and admired her. Some of her letters were published in 1838, the remainder in 1888, and they have remained a connoisseur's delight ever since.

There are so many other memorable writers remembered mostly for their letters that it is difficult to list more than a few, but a short list would certainly include Lady Mary Wortley Montagu (1689–1762), and Mme de Sévigné, mentioned earlier.

Other, less aristocratic women wrote under circumstances less congenial to even this degree of literary expression. The recently discovered journal of Anne Hughes has been published as *The Diary of a Farmer's Wife, 1796–97*.[4] Anne Hughes, who apparently had a decent but not an extensive education, records the daily life of a prosperous farm, including the activities and moods of her husband, who emerges clearly as a personality for the reader. She describes him with fondness, as basically a good man and a good husband, but he is also at times a 'big silly', as he tends to lose his temper over trifles.

Anne Hughes was evidently a woman at peace with life, but her diary nevertheless has poignant moments. In her rather male-dominated world, she learns to value the company of her maid, sees to it that the girl is trained and educated as her talents allow, and rejoices at her marriage to the local parson, while at the same time regretting the loss of her close companion. Women alone on farms will know what it means to have another woman close by. More striking, for our purposes, is the fact that Anne conceals her diary from her husband, evidently feeling that somehow he would not approve, but treasuring opportunities to use her pen. When she learns that she is pregnant, she resolutely puts the diary away for good, understanding that in future she will have no time to devote to it. It is hard to believe that she led a lonely and frustrated life thereafter, but as modern readers we feel sympathy for a woman who, for all her prosperity, could not even allow herself the modest but highly cherished degree of self-expression her diary represented.

Among other diarists whose work is memorable are Hester Thrale (1741–1821), friend of Samuel Johnson; Dorothy Wordsworth (1771–1855), sister of the poet William; and Alice James (1842–92), sister of Henry and William. All of these are women who had considerable literary talents and even ambitions, but in one way or another felt overshadowed by famous men close to them, and put their greatest energies into more 'private' literary activities.

The autobiographies of women who made their main contributions in fields other than literature often have a special fascination. Simone de Beauvoir (1908–87) did write some novels, but she will probably best be remembered for her monumental *The Second Sex* (1949, translated 1953), a pioneering, encyclopedic work of feminist scholarship written at a time when feminism seemed to be in hibernation. Although some of its analyses are dated, and many apply best to French conditions, it is still essential reading for anyone interested in the basics of feminist thought. De Beauvoir was one of the leading French Existentialists in the middle of the century, the close companion of Jean-Paul Sartre, and, in addition to philosophical works, she produced four fascinating volumes of autobiography which chart both her own progress and that of a whole generation of internationally influential French thinkers. The aptly titled *Memoirs of a Dutiful Daughter* (1959) indicates her starting point, but she is unique in having recorded virtually her whole life, from childhood to old age, all seen personally but also analysed socially and politically through her powerful critical intellect.

Other memorable autobiographers are Vera Brittain, whose *Testament of Youth* (1933) records in often moving terms the social and emotional devastation of World War One; Mary McCarthy, whose *Memories of a Catholic Girlhood* (1957) includes the most memorable uncle of the century; and Maya Angelou, whose *I Know Why the Caged Bird Sings* (1970) conveys, often humorously but also painfully, what it was like to grow up as a poor black in the southern United States.

A final category of 'non-literary' writing which has received increased attention in the past few years is travel writing – not only that by women, to be sure, but readers have often been surprised to realize how many women have set out on exotic, dangerous, demanding, often solitary journeys, apparently either defying convention or feeling utterly indifferent to it. Some have virtually made careers out of travelling and writing about it.

Often such women had the financial support, and perhaps the self-confidence, provided by a privileged background, but one of the most noted of our contemporaries is the Irish Dervla

Murphy (1931–   ), who came from modest circumstances and chose (partly from sheer necessity) to travel by bicycle. Her first journey took her from Dublin to India by way of the Himalayas and Afghanistan, and resulted in the enthusiastic, freshly observed *High Tilt* (1965). Murphy later went on to new parts of the globe, including Ethiopia, Peru and Madagascar, and she also returned to certain countries to explore further. A feature that makes some of her later books particularly individual is that she began to take her young daughter along on her cycling tours; on the first occasion she visited India with a child who was only four years old.

As Murphy's experience indicates, a woman traveller often experiences aspects of a culture unavailable to a man; it is a point that anthropologists have long been aware of. A woman travelling alone with a young child is even more interestingly placed, as the child forces her into a degree of settled domestic life that a lone adult would probably bypass. In *On a Shoestring to Coorg* (1976), for example, Murphy and her daughter live for various periods in different parts of southern India, and come to understand in detail the differences within the region. At one point they attend a wedding, and between them they are encouraged to participate in different aspects of the festivities. Dervla Murphy is still travelling and writing constantly, and her further adventures are worth watching out for.

In general one should also keep an open mind, and an eye out, for writings by women which do not appear to fit into pre-ordained categories. Perhaps women, even today feeling they have less stake in the literary establishment than men do, will feel freer to write in forms and genres that suit their experience; certainly many women of the past gave their talents outlets in whatever forms came to hand.

7 Women's Writing: Integrated or Segregated?

Throughout this book, we have been considering writing by individual women authors mostly in relation to writing by other women, although we have occasionally referred to writing by men to explain the circumstances under which women wrote and were read. A question that is frequently asked is whether it is really satisfactory to study women's writing in such isolation in the long run.

Certainly such an approach, if practised rigidly, may create difficulties. It may obscure the extent to which women writers were influenced by men, and the extent to which they participated in the literary movements of their time which have already been charted, but with emphasis previously given to the contributions of male writers.

In addition, if women's writing is looked at in isolation, those who wrote mostly or exclusively about women may be given prominence, on the perhaps unexamined grounds that considering women as subject matter justifies considering only women writers. A real danger is that those whose subject matter is more varied or more general may tend to be ignored; in the academic context, they may suffer from being studied neither in courses on women's writing, nor in other courses (where their work has already long been underrepresented.)

In colleges and universities, one now often finds optional courses devoted to women writers. In most places, although such courses are open to all students, they are chosen largely or exclusively by women students, and they are most often taught by women teachers. This situation may tend to create an academic 'ghetto' for women's writing, and to reinforce the already existing prejudice to the effect that it is a specialized or minority interest, not a part of the main stream.

Most scholars and teachers engaged in the study of women's writing would nevertheless argue that studying women's writing as a special topic is necessary, at least as an interim measure. Such special study has already helped to focus attention on, and 'revive', undeservedly neglected writers and works. It also provides a basis for the scholarship necessary to create and explore the 'history' of women's writing. Feminist approaches to literary study can conveniently be introduced in this context. Historical and critical approaches learned in studying women's writing can give both students and teachers a basis for challenging received notions about literature encountered in other contexts. This experience helps to make possible a long-term re-evaluation of our idea of 'English literature', an evaluation that is agreed to be necessary even by many who are not particularly interested in women's literature as such.

Most specialists on women's writing would however agree that it is not *sufficient* to provide separate academic courses on women's writing. These should exist parallel with a conscious attempt to introduce texts by women into other courses, especially introductory ones, and feminist critical approaches should be a natural element of any teaching of literature. As increasing numbers of students, both women and men, are exposed to such approaches, and as critics and scholars, both women and men, extend their familiarity with women's writing, the danger of creating a ghetto should be eliminated.

The sex of the writer is only one of many facts worth knowing about a literary work. What we must strive to avoid is a situation in which our awareness of the sex of the writer conditions all of our other responses to the work. Not least, we must try to avoid returning to a situation in which knowing that a text is by a woman is a justification for ignoring it.

NOTES

Chapter 1

[1] London, Faber & Faber, 1975, pp. 185–6.
[2] In Chapter 4. (London, Hogarth Press, 1929), p. 111. There are many later editions of *A Room of One's Own*.
[3] A study by Elaine Showalter, cited by Cheri Register in 'American Feminist Literary Criticism: A Bibliographical Introduction', in Josephine Donovan, (ed.), *Feminist Literary Criticism* (Lexington, University of Kentucky Press, 1975), pp. 14–15.
[4] Chapter 4, p. 115
[5] Chapter 5, pp. 157–8.

Chapter 2

[1] See Carol Ohmann, 'Emily Brontë in the Hands of Male Critics', in Mary Eagleton, (ed.), *Feminist Literary Theory: A Reader* (Oxford, Basil Blackwell, 1986), pp. 71–4. Originally published in *College English*, vol. 32, no. 8, May 1971.
[2] 'The Impact of Feminism on the Theatre', in Eagleton, *Feminist Literary Theory*, pp. 104–5. Originally published in *Feminist Review*, no. 18.

Chapter 3

[1] In *Salt and Bitter and Good: Three Centuries of English and American Women Poets* (London and New York, Paddington Press, 1975).

Chapter 4

[1] See Ian Watt, *The Rise of the Novel*, (London, Chatto & Windus, 1957), especially Chapters 1 and 2.
[2] Spencer, (Oxford, Basil Blackwell); Spender, (London, Pandora).
[3] Chapter 5. *Northanger Abbey* was written in 1803 but not published until 1818.
[4] Letter to Anna Austen, 9 September 1814.
[5] Letter to J. Edward Austen, 16 December 1816.

[6] Chapter 12.

[7] Chapter 8.

[8] Chapter 23.

[9] Chapter 34.

[10] Gerd Bjørhovde. *Rebellious Structures: Women Writers and the Crisis of the Novel 1880–1900* (London, Oxford University Press, 1987).

[11] *Deadlock*, in *Pilgrimage 3* (London, Virago, 1979), pp. 50–1.

[12] In 'Dorothy Richardson', in *Women and Writing*, (London, The Women's Press, 1979), pp. 189 and 190. Originally published in a review of *The Tunnel* in 1919.

[13] Op cit, p. 191.

[14] 'Modern Fiction', in *The Common Reader: First Series* (London, Hogarth Press, reprinted 1968), p. 104. Originally published in 1919.

[15] See, for example, Elaine Showalter, *The Female Malady* (London, Virago, 1987).

[16] See especially Carolyn Heilburn, *Towards Androgyny: Aspects of Male and Female in Literature* (London, Victor Gollancz, 1973).

[17] See 'An Interview with Margaret Drabble', conducted by Nancy S. Hardin, *Contemporary Literature*, vol. 14, no. 3, p. 277.

Chapter 5

[1] *A Room of One's Own*, Chapter 4, p. 98.

[2] Interview, cited in Michelene Wandor, *Understudies: Theatre and Sexual Politics* (London, Methuen, 1981), p. 63.

[3] London, Samuel French, 1977, p. 43.

Chapter 6

[1] 'Dorothy Osborne's Letters', in *The Common Reader: Second Series*, (London, Hogarth Press, reprinted 1965), p. 60. Originally published in 1932.

[2] Dorothy Osborne, *Letters to William Temple*, ed. Kenneth Parker (London, Penguin, 1987), pp. 89–90. (Text normalized).

[3] Op cit, p. 109 (Text normalized).

[4] Jeanne Preston, (ed.) (Harmondsworth, Penguin, 1981).

8 FURTHER READING

In addition to the works cited in the text, the following can be recommended. This is only a small selection; bibliographies and references in them will help you to find critical works on individual writers.

Feminist theory

Simone de Beauvoir, *The Second Sex* (Harmondsworth, Penguin, 1972 and later reprints).
> A monument, it provides central concepts of modern feminism and also offers the first 'images of women' criticism of male writers.

Feminist literary history

There has been much more work done on women novelists than on any other group; doubtless the prestige of the major women novelists of the nineteenth century lies behind this fact.

Eva Figes, *Sex and Subterfuge: Women Writers to 1850* (London, Macmillan, 1982).
> How women shaped the novel for their own purposes.

Sandra M. Gilbert and Susan Gubar, *The Madwoman in the Attic: The Women Writer and the Nineteenth Century Literary Imagination* (New Haven, Conn., Yale University Press, 1979).
> Discusses factors which made writing a source of anxiety for many women.

Jane Miller, *Women Writing About Men* (London, Virago, 1986).
> An inversion of the 'images of women' approach. What do women see in men – and why?

Ellen Moers, *Literary Women: The Great Writers* (London, The Women's Press, 1978).

Gives accounts of women who regarded writing as a profession, some of whom wrote in languages other than English.

Elaine Showalter, *A Literature of their Own: British Women Novelists from Brontë to Lessing* Second revised edition. (London, Virago, 1984).

Attempts to establish the existence of a 'women's tradition' in literature, ignored by conventional literary histories.

Feminist literary criticism and theory

Mary Eagleton (ed.), *Feminist Literary Theory* (Oxford and New York, Basil Blackwell, 1986).

Gives excerpts from many key texts, including several reflecting recent French theory.

Mary Ellmann, *Thinking About Women* (London, Virago, 1979). (First published 1969.)

Non-polemical but original musings on how women are represented in writing.

Kate Millett, *Sexual Politics* (London, Virago, 1977). (First published 1970.)

Not about women writers, but one of the first texts in English to examine the depiction of women in fictional works by men from a feminist standpoint.

Toril Moi, *Sexual/Textual Politics: Feminist Literary Theory* (London, Methuen, 1985).

Provides an introduction to recent French theory as well as to Anglo-American approaches.

Joanna Russ, *How to Suppress Women's Writing* (London, The Women's Press, 1984).

Entertaining but sharp account of the obstacles to acceptance and preservation of writing by women.

Elaine Showalter (ed.), *The New Feminist Criticism: Essays on Women, Literature and Theory* (London, Virago, 1986).

Gives full texts of several recent, central essays not previously published in book form. Excellent bibliography.

Index